PORTRAIT OF
THE WORDSWORTH COUNTRY

Portrait of
THE WORDSWORTH COUNTRY

by

Ronald Sands

ROBERT HALE · LONDON

FOR JASON, CLAIRE, AILSA AND IONA

The Child is father of the Man;
And I could wish my days to be
Bound each to each by natural piety.

© *Ronald Sands 1984*
First published in Great Britain 1984

ISBN 0 7090 1739 1

Robert Hale Limited
Clerkenwell House
Clerkenwell Green
London EC1R 0HT

Photoset by Rowland Phototypesetting Ltd
Printed in Great Britain by
St Edmundsbury Press, Bury St Edmunds, Suffolk
Bound by Hunter and Foulis Ltd

Contents

Illustrations

All photographs were taken especially for this book by John Bunch

Acknowledgements

A book of this kind owes an immense debt to many people and I freely acknowledge my gratitude to the authors and editors of the various works I have consulted and quoted from. All these works are fully listed in the Bibliography, but I must make special mention of the Oxford University Press, not only for providing excellent popular editions of the works of William and Dorothy Wordsworth but also for publishing in recent years newly revised editions of the Wordsworth Letters under the inspired general editorship of Alan G. Hill.

The staff and administrators of the various Wordsworth properties open to the public also deserve special mention. Day after day, year after year, they keep alive the reputation and example of what has come to be known as the 'Wordsworth Circle'. I have been so greatly assisted by so many people connected with these properties that I hope they will forgive me for not singling out any particular persons for special commendation. In any case, the properties are fully described in the text and I rejoice to see each one flourishing: the Birthplace at Cockermouth; Hawkshead School; the Wordsworth Rooms at Windebrowe; Dove Cottage, Grasmere and its associated Wordsworth Library and Wordsworth Museum; Rydal Mount; St Oswald's Church, Grasmere. All these institutions need and deserve our support. I should also like to thank the staff of the Cumbria Library Service at Ambleside, Kendal and Windermere.

My greatest personal debt in writing this book belongs to John Bunch whose impressive photography and endless patience on our many Wordsworthian excursions are beyond praise. Finally I record my thanks to the late Ethel Jane Hartley for her ancient but trusty typewriter.

Preface

When local government reorganization merged the former counties of Cumberland and Westmorland and the Furness part of Lancashire into one large county, there was much discussion concerning the name for this 'new' area. Today most people accept the revival of the ancient term 'Cumbria' for the enlarged county, but the name 'Wordsworthshire' might have had an almost equal claim, for by the end of Wordsworth's long life there were few parts of Cumbria which were unknown to him and his family. Certainly no other single person has been responsible for spreading the fame of this region to all corners of the world.

'Wordsworthshire ... Wordsworthshire ... Wordsworthshire ...' Repeat the word a few times aloud. Better still, place it in an imaginary but emphatic context: 'My aunt lives in Wordsworthshire' or 'I am going up to Wordsworthshire for the weekend.' We can almost believe that there really is such a sublime and beautiful county in the far north-west of England. 'Sublime and Beautiful' – the very words Wordsworth himself used to describe this unique area.

It is truly remarkable, perhaps miraculous, that so much of the region which this book explores has remained unspoilt. Join me in the steps of our distinguished poet and I can promise you at the very least a fascinating and varied journey. And at journey's end you might be granted that heaven-sent ability to recollect in tranquillity the landscape and experiences which inspired some of the finest poetry in English and assert with our poet that

> There was a time when meadow, grove, and stream,
> The earth, and every common sight,
> > To me did seem
> > Apparelled in celestial light,
> The glory and the freshness of a dream.

11

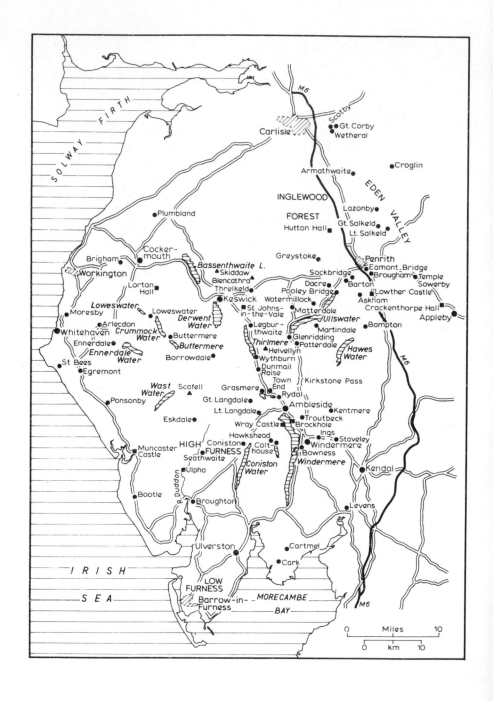

1

'Where Once the Dove and Olive Bough . . .'

Dove Cottage and its surroundings

Many people find it deeply ironic that Wordsworth, the great exponent of 'plain living and high thinking', should have made his home in a house which had once been an inn. The very name 'Dove Cottage' harks back to the days when weary travellers could refresh themselves at the 'Dove and Olive Branch'. He wryly refers to the former use of his home:

> . . . where the Dove and Olive-bough
> Once hung, a Poet harbours now,
> A simple, water-drinking Bard . . . .

It was a happy home, but also, perforce, a frugal one. When Walter Scott stayed, he complained good-humouredly that they served only three meals a day at Dove Cottage, and two of those consisted of oats. There is a strong local tradition that Scott would lock the door of his room, climb secretly out of the window and make for the Swan Hotel, where he would enjoy a more hearty breakfast washed down with Scotch whisky. Indeed, there is a more refined version of the story which asserts that when Scott paid a visit to the hotel with members of the Dove Cottage household, they were all puzzled as to why he should be greeted by both staff and locals at the inn as if they were old friends.

But if the Wordsworths denied themselves much alcohol, they could certainly drink in a superb view of the lake, for at this period the row of cottages in front of the house had not been built, and a splendidly uninterrupted panorama could be enjoyed across to the opposite shore. There is also a suggestion that Grasmere Lake was at a higher level in the early nineteenth century and consequently came much closer to the cottage. Another major change since that time is that the house was then on the main road, which went over White Moss, the present A591 not having yet been built.

Wordsworth had first noticed the cottage on a walking tour with Samuel Taylor Coleridge a few weeks before they moved in. He wrote to Dorothy: 'There is a small house at Grasmere empty which perhaps we will take, and purchase furniture but of this we will speak.' He also harboured a plan to build his own cottage, much impressed by the story of a Devonshire man who had built his own house for £130. This ambition to build recurs throughout his life, but it was to remain unfulfilled.

Their income amounted to £80 per year at this time – interest on a legacy left to them by Raisley Calvert of Windebrowe near Keswick. Although not a princely sum, it was still twice the average local wage at the turn of the century. Consequently their lifestyle at Town End, whilst not by any means lavish, was still better than most people could afford.

Only later was the house named Dove Cottage; in the Wordsworths' day it was simply referred to by the name of the hamlet, Town End.

Wordsworth and his sister Dorothy arrived at what one might think to be an unpropitious time of the year – late December. It was a mistake they never repeated, their three other house moves being conducted in the more favourable month of May or June. Not that they seemed to mind the harshness of the season, for there were celebrations immediately ahead of them: Dorothy's twenty-eighth birthday on the 25th made Christmas a double celebration throughout their lives, and a week later they were to celebrate a notable New Year, as they said farewell to the eighteenth century and welcomed the nineteenth, for they first arrived at Town End on Friday 20 December 1799. But it was not the birthday that excited them, nor even a century turning, but their boundless delight at being together again in a permanent home, something they had barely experienced since early childhood.

This excitement comes through in the letters in which they later recalled their first arrival at the obscure cottage which now greets some ninety thousand visitors each year: 'We found no preparations except beds without curtains in the rooms upstairs and a dying spark in the grate of the gloomy parlour, but we were young and healthy and had attained an object long desired. We had returned to our native mountains there to live.' But if Dorothy's recollection makes their arrival seem lonely and forlorn, she quickly settled down: 'We are daily more delighted with Grasmere and its neighbourhood; our walks are perpetually varied, and we are more fond of the mountains as our acquaintance with them encreases.'

Brother and sister were soon part of the local community, and their new neighbours, though anxious not to pry or interfere, were no doubt keeping a friendly if curious eye on the newcomers. When some years later de Quincey took over the tenancy of the property, he was much amused to discover on arrival that the locals had already learned a good deal about him, not least the fact that he was an eligible bachelor of some means. There is no reason to doubt that the 'Town Enders' in 1799 were any the less curious or well informed.

One of the Wordsworths' close neighbours was Molly Fisher of nearby Syke Side, who became their devoted daily help. She recalled years later how Dorothy had arrived dressed in a striped gown and straw bonnet. During the four years or so that Molly helped the growing family, she became a great favourite not only with the Wordsworths but with their many distinguished visitors and guests, among them some of the leading intellectuals of the day. Coleridge referred to her as 'a drollery belonging to the cottage', but they never despised her for her simple ways and lack of education; her devotion and kindness were too obvious to make her the butt of cruel jokes. But Hazlitt could not forbear to observe that she was the only woman in England who, ten years after the French Revolution, still did not know that it had taken place.

The family were relieved that Molly could be their daily help and would not require full board and accommodation. She was happy to serve them for two shillings a week, and for that she did chores such as lighting fires and washing dishes. She served them loyally until 1804, when she was obliged to leave to look after her brother. By this time, however, Wordsworth was rather pleased to see her go without having to dismiss her, for her strength and faculties had begun to fail. But her 'promotion' to the position of her brother's housekeeper on the death of his wife seems to have given her a new lease of life. She quickly transformed Syke Side – one of the untidiest and dirtiest houses in Grasmere, according to Dorothy – into one of the cleanest. She remained close to the Wordsworths, constantly bringing them treats such as a basin of gooseberries or a few curds and the odd pound of butter from the cow she had in her charge. She also entertained the Wordsworth children, over-indulging them with her cream porridge.

As one enters Dove Cottage through a rugged stone porch with its tiny slate seat (a boon for patiently waiting visitors on a rainy day), the first room one sees is the 'houseplace' or kitchen-parlour, dating from the early part of the seventeenth century. Usually in this room there is a roaring friendly fire, in warm contrast to that dying spark in the grate which William and Dorothy found on their arrival. The rag rug in front of the fire on the floor of stone flags adds to the homeliness of the cosy room. The tiny diamond-paned window lets in little light, and the dark oak wainscotting (a relic from the days when this was a public house) makes the room seem gloomy even on the brightest day. But there is always a welcoming cosiness, and despite the tens of thousands of visitors who pass through the room each year, one can still feel that one has dropped in on the Wordsworths only to find them out in the garden or rowing on the lake. This friendly atmosphere is a tribute to the staff who care for the property, taking great pains to ensure that the rooms are always impeccably clean and having fires in at least two rooms on all but the sultriest days. Indeed, making the fire on any particular day is not merely an extra chore for the staff: it is considered a privilege. They must be grateful, though, that they do not have to use the tinderbox on display in an adjoining room. William was vastly pleased with this innovation, but poor Molly, whose task it was to try to kindle a flame by this painstaking method, maintained that, if you did not strike fire after forty minutes, you struck blood.

Above the houseplace fire hangs a framed print which has the distinction of being the only item on display which the Wordsworths could never have seen or have been associated with. But before the historical purists demand that the intruding item be removed, they should bear in mind that the bewhiskered Victorian gentleman in the photograph is the Reverend Stopford Brooke, who was instrumental, as long ago as 1890, in forming a Trust to acquire Dove Cottage and open it to the public.

On the wall opposite is a painting which captures the very heart of day-to-day life at Town End: it is a large canvas showing Pepper, the dog presented to the Wordsworths by Walter Scott. By Pepper's portrait is the framed certificate of appointment which Wordsworth received from Queen Victoria on becoming Poet Laureate. This belongs to a period of his life many years after he had left Dove Cottage, but its quaint usage of English makes absorbing reading:

> These are to require you to swear and admit William Wordsworth Esquire into the Place and Quality of Poet Laureate to Her Majesty in the room of Robert Southey Esquire deceased. To have hold exercise and enjoy the said place together with all rights profits privileges and advantages thereunto belonging into as full and ample manner as the said Robert Southey Esquire did hold and enjoy or of right ought to have held and enjoyed the same and for so doing this shall be your warrant given under my hand and seal this sixth day of April 1843 in the Sixth Year of Her Majesty's Reign.

The adjoining room also belies the house's original purpose, for again the walls are faced with dark oak wainscotting. This was used as a bedroom: at first by Dorothy and later by William, and later still by William and his wife Mary. They put down matting in an attempt to insulate the cold floor, though the room today is very cosy with its bright fire, which would have been fuelled both by blocks of peat cut locally and by sea coal from Whitehaven. To the left of the fireplace is a pile of nicely dried blocks of peat, and close by a cupboard at floor level reveals a store of sea coal.

Next to this is a built-in cupboard, large enough to stand in, and here they would have stored the food items which needed to be kept dry – tea, coffee and, presumably a prize possession, the barrel 'of the best flour' which a friend had sent them from America. Some of this Dorothy used on arrival to make, rather unsuccessfully, some pepper cake – the gingerbread for which Grasmere is still famed and which is still on sale in the village.

Perhaps too it was this enormous barrel of flour which proved so tempting to the local rats, for a cat had to be acquired to keep the pests at bay. This unromantic but highly practical reason for keeping one of Creation's most beautiful pets is hardly the most appropriate topic for a poem of the kind associated with Wordsworth, but watching the kitten chasing leaves with his baby daughter on his knee, he was much delighted by the spectacle:

> – But the kitten, how she starts,
> Crouches, stretches, paws, and darts!
> With a tiger-leap half way
> Now she meets the coming prey. . . .

Such a favourite must have been well looked after, no doubt sharing the fresh milk which their cow provided. At one stage they also kept a pig. But most of their food seems to have been plain and simple, with fresh vegetables from the garden, and oats were a staple ingredient of many meals. The number of times Dorothy records baking pies suggests that these were either popular or economical.

She is more revealing than she realizes when she records the humour they all enjoyed at hearing some of baby John's first words – 'pie and tates', meaning pie and potatoes. But apparently he used this phrase as a generic description of *all* food, suggesting that these simple, filling items were often to be found on the dining-table at the cottage.

Above the fireplace is a portrait of Florence, the daughter of Thomas de Quincey, who took over the tenancy after the Wordsworths left. His collection of eighty thousand books must certainly have given credence to the maxim that books do furnish a room. In the case of de Quincey, they must have furnished the whole house.

The most striking piece of furniture in the room is a set of drawers with a cabinet at either end incorporating washbowls, enabling it to be used simultaneously by two people. Apparently the water they washed in would be recycled: that is to say, it was poured into a jug after use and saved to be used again.

A small larder leads off one side of the room, lined with shelves and, recently, crammed with apples which gave off a most pleasing aroma. But the most noticeable aspect of the larder is the immediate and dramatic drop in temperature. This coolness is due partly to the fact that a branch of the beck actually runs under the stone-flagged floor.

Back in the warmth of the main room again, there are some more interesting items on the walls: a framed silhouette of Dorothy in her youth, the only known likeness of her from her early life; a silhouette of Sara Hutchinson, the 'Asra' of Coleridge's poems; and a small, late portrait of Mary Wordsworth, looking kindly but somewhat gaunt and showing signs of that 'considerable obliquity of vision' noticed by De Quincey.

The ceilings of both these ground-floor rooms are low. Add to this the already tiny dimensions of the rooms and it is easy to understand why the family soon began to complain of being overcrowded. Today visitors are taken round in groups of fifteen at the maximum, partly because of the small size of the cottage but also to maintain the intimacy of the experience which the staff and trustees rightly value so highly. This can mean that, in the busy period of high summer, some waiting is necessary as groups are conducted around the house. The staff work a clever rota which ensures that, whilst three or four groups may be being conducted around, one barely glimpses another as a party moves from room to room. Military precision and theatrical timing are very much in evidence.

But if fifteen people standing up and simply passing briefly through each room are as much as the property can stand, how frustrating it must have been for the occupants, as their family increased and grew, and as more and more guests dropped in. In addition to Dorothy, Mary and William, there were three children born here: John (1803), Dora (1804) and Thomas (1806). When they left for Allan Bank in the summer of 1808, Mary was again with child. Their visitors, too, were not simply 'callers' but might stay days and weeks at a time. Coleridge would sit round the fire talking until the early hours of the morning, and other visitors included Walter Scott, John Wordsworth, Sara Hutchinson and the Southeys. Dorothy describes a typical Christmas when they traditionally had a visit from the Grasmere fiddler: 'I have been summoned into the kitchen to dance with Johnny and I have danced until I am out of Breath . . . a pleasant sound they make with their little pattering feet on the stone floor, half a dozen of them, Boys and Girls. . . .'

From this room creaking stairs lead upwards, a climb often accompanied by the sound of the cuckoo clock, a gift to Wordsworth on his seventieth birthday when the family were living at Rydal Mount which was received with a great deal of glee. Mary wrote: '. . . no children were ever more delighted with a new toy than we are with the subject of it. Dear Miss Wordsworth was seated before it upon the top of the stairs the other day – and when the bird had performed its office, and the little door flopped to, I thought she would have dropped from her chair, she laughed so heartilly at the sudden exit of the little mimic.' William even found the sound therapeutic, and far from its interfering with his sleep, he maintained that it

soothed him when he was restless and mingled pleasantly
with his dreams when he was fast asleep:

> List, Cuckoo – Cuckoo! – oft tho' tempests howl,
> Or nipping frosts remind thee trees are bare,
> How cattle pine, and droop the shivering fowl,
> Thy spirits will seem to feed on balmy air:
> I speak with knowledge, – by that Voice beguiled,
> Thou wilt salute old memories as they throng
> Into thy heart; and fancies, running wild
> Through fresh green fields, and budding groves among,
> Will make thee happy, happy as a child;
> Of sunshine wilt thou think, and flowers, and song,
> And breathe as in a world where nothing can go wrong.

On a really quiet day in the cottage the loud ticking of
the clock can be heard in every room: with three noisy
children playing in the house, one can only marvel that
some of the finest poems in English were written, revised
and refined here by William, with a great deal of help from
his 'amanuenses' Mary and Dorothy, who acted as unpaid
secretaries and scribes. They also clearly inspired him on
many occasions, and he frequently drew upon Dorothy's
descriptions and observations.

Half-way up the stairs, a door has been constructed to
allow direct access to the garden. This was added at
Wordsworth's behest, on the suggestion of a friend. They
never regretted the improvement, which continues to be a
boon today, as it enables a partial one-way system to
operate, as visitors walk round the house and finish in the
garden.

The room on the right is of special significance as it was
the main sitting-room which, in the days before the building of the houses opposite, enjoyed views across the Lake,
with Silver Howe prominent. Here they might drink coffee, freshly ground in the implement which resembles a
meat-grinder in the room downstairs; or, if they felt really
extravagant, they would drink tea, something of an expensive luxury in those days, compared with coffee. Perhaps
too, they would take breakfast here: Dorothy recalls
William composing one of the 'Butterfly poems' at such an

early morning meal '. . . with his basin of broth before him untouched, and a little plate of bread and butter . . .'. If parents of teenaged children sometimes despair of their offspring's *déshabillé* at breakfast, they might find a crumb of comfort in Dorothy's description of the dress of the future Poet Laureate as he penned his verse: 'He ate not a morsel, nor put on his stockings, but sate with his shirt neck unbuttoned, and his waist coat open . . .' But on this occasion he seems at least to have had a modicum of peace and quiet. When the bad weather of 1807–8 prevented his usual practice of composing out of doors, Dorothy comments on his application: 'I cannot but admire the fortitude and wonder at the success with which he has laboured in that one room, common to all the family, to all visitors, and where the children frequently played beside him. . . .' Dorothy also writes eloquently of that peculiar form of silence which falls upon a house at night when the noisy children have been despatched to their beds. William, similarly, paints a vivid vignette in verse, comparing silence favourably with small talk:

> Better than such discourse doth silence long,
> Long barren silence, square with my desire;
> To sit without emotion, hope or aim,
> In the loved presence of my cottage-fire,
> And listen to the flapping of the flame,
> Or kettle whispering its faint undersong.

Also in this 'half-kitchen, half-parlour' are some interesting portraits. Over the fireplace is the delicately tinted portrait by Henry Edridge, made when the poet was thirty-six and a great favourite with Wordsworth scholars as it shows him at a time when he was writing some of his most-admired work in this very room. By then he had written 'The Prelude', published a second edition of *Lyrical Ballads*, and had dotted the final 'i's and crossed the final 't's of one of his masterpieces – 'Ode; Intimations of Immortality from Recollections of Early Childhood'. Well may he stare out from this portrait looking assured, confident, experienced, and showing too, perhaps, the kind of maturity which is born of living through a personal tragedy: the death the year before of his beloved brother John, drowned in a shipwreck off the coast of Dorset.

On the opposite wall is an excellent reproduction in colour of a portrait of Wordsworth, less well-known since it is owned by that hive of Wordsworthian scholarship, Cornell University in New York State. This is the Shuter portrait made when he was twenty-eight years old, in 1798, a year before he came to Dove Cottage and the year in which he wrote another of his greatest poems, 'Lines Composed a Few Miles Above Tintern Abbey'. The face is fuller, more youthful and more tanned, and the eyes look out with a visionary gleam of one who can assert:

> . . . And I have felt
> A presence that disturbs me with the joy
> Of elevated thoughts; a sense sublime
> Of something far more deeply interfused,
> Whose dwelling is the light of setting suns,
> And the round ocean and the living air,
> And the blue sky, and in the mind of man.

And finally, to complete the panoply of portraits, there is one by Benjamin Haydon done in 1818 when Wordsworth was forty-eight. Here the eyes look away, up to our left, the hair is receding and greying, there are crows' feet around the eyes, and the lower cheek and chin show unmistakable signs of middle age. There is still great strength and conviction in the face, but strength and conviction of a different order compared with the earlier portraits. The painting belongs to a year in which his life was dominated by local politics and an obsessive desire to ensure that the Lowther Tory cause triumphed in the Westmorland Parliamentary election of that year.

These three single portraits of Wordsworth at different stages of his early and middle life are counterpointed by a painting showing him seated at a table with his wife. Although a studied, almost theatrically arranged painting, it was one which justly pleased the family and which will no doubt gain more admirers in the wake of the discovery of the long-lost love-letters they had exchanged in their earlier life together. The detail and rich colouring of this miniature by Margaret Gillies are almost magical, as are the effects of light and shade she achieved. A serenity suffuses the whole scene. Canon Rawnsley related an amusing anecdote about the completion of this work: Miss Gillies 'had finished the portrait, and her trunk was packed; the chaise was at the door when, in the silence, she heard the loud booming voice of the bard on the landing upstairs, enquiring of his wife with all solemnity, "My dear, would it be considered very indecorous or profligate if I gave Miss Gillies a kiss at parting?" She did not hear the rejoinder but supposed that Mrs Wordsworth had assented. At any rate she left Rydal Mount with the poet's kiss on her brow, and a chuckle in her heart.' A similar portrait can be seen at Rydal Mount.

The three chairs have seats embroidered by daughters of three poets and are accordingly initialled by them – Dora Wordsworth, Sara Coleridge and Edith Southey. William's daughter-in-law, Fanny, made the knee-rug from wool which she had gathered locally and knitted herself; she also dyed the cover, ingeniously using a variety of vegetable colourings which are listed on a card nearby; some twenty-two different colours were produced by mixing tin, chrome, alum or tannic acid with a variety of vegetable sources, including cow parsley, broom, bilberries, begonias, boxwood bark, lichens, privet berries and rhubarb. And if this were not more than enough to make this room unique, the couch on which the shawl rests might even be the very one on which Wordsworth lay 'in vacant or in pensive mood'.

A cabinet contains a number of personal items, including the ice-skates he used, and a silver-based medal dated 1848 inscribed 'William Wordsworth' and around the edge 'Friend of the wise and teacher of the good'.

The room containing the curtained bed (originally in Rydal Mount) contains Wordsworth's passport in a hinged, double-sided glass frame. Issued by the French Government in 1836, the document is in French and is headed '*AU NOM DU ROI*'. A list of physical characteristics reveals that Wordsworth's forehead was bald, his eyes and hair grey, his complexion ordinary, his chin round, his face oval and his nose (a fact at variance with his portraits) medium. The stamps and permissions to enter certain states and countries read like an index to an historical atlas and include a number of countries which no longer exist. Tuscany, Rome, Milan, Naples, Belgium, Sardinia, Venice, Nice and the Papal Authority are all separately mentioned.

In the windowseat is a battered and much-used portmanteau on which Wordsworth carved his name and the date 1820. Some thirty-five years before, when he similarly carved his name on a desk at his Hawkshead school, he must have had either more room or a better eye, for this particular carving ran out of space before his name was complete and it reads:

H
W WORDSWORT

Among the pictures on the wall is one of special interest painted by Dora and showing the outside of Dove Cottage in their day. The yew tree by the cottage is still growing, but the distinctive vertical flagstones forming the wall in front of the garden have now gone. But similar fences can be seen near the church in Hawkshead and in Ambleside. The distinguished historical geographer and author Dr William Rollinson has made a special study of the different types of stone walls in Lakeland and asserts that this particular method is very localized, being related to the geological nature of the area in which he has found them: Coniston, Hawkshead, Ambleside and the Lickle Valley, all places where the Brathay Flags outcrop.

Looking east, with an excellent view of the garden, is a room which Dorothy in 1800 called the lumber room and in 1805 'the pantry, lumber room etc'. How useful such a multi-purpose but ill-defined room must have been to the growing family. Some doubt exists, however, about the precise nature of the uses of this room and, as if to hedge their bets, the Trustees have furnished it very sparsely indeed.

This and the other main upstairs rooms have nicely decorated walls, and the whole of the cottage is kept truly spick and span. But in one of the rooms downstairs a small area of paintwork has been left exposed above the fireplace. This probably gives a more accurate idea of the decor of the period: somewhat smoke-stained, dark yellow walls. If the small fireplace in the lumber room was in regular use, its walls must also have been much darkened by smoke, not improved by the using of home-made tallow candles and rush-lights.

In one corner of the lumber room a glass cabinet contains items of interest – most strikingly the Chinese druggist's balance marked 'T de Q' and a small blue stone, irregularly shaped and the size of a penny piece. A label tells the extraordinary use to which this stone was put, in the words of Sara Hutchinson (1826): 'I must tell you that Mr W's eyes have been cured by one of our visitors, Mr Reynolds, who prescribed touching them with a blue stone which acted like magic on them.'

There is also a polished wooden cask with brass handles and decorative legs used as a tea-caddy. Significantly, for tea was a great luxury, there is a lock on the box. The Wordsworths were connoisseurs of tea, and in later life Dorothy became friendly with the Twining daughters and breakfasted with them when in London. The name Twining, of course, is still associated with fine teas, one of the few commodities which is immeasurably cheaper today than a century ago. On a visit to Lady Beaumont in Leicestershire, Dorothy once paced around the coach stop *en route* to her destination, desperately longing for the tea which was on offer but feeling unable to afford this seemingly extravagant luxury. In better-off days, she ran up bills at Twinings for as much as £26 for such delights as Pekoe and Souchang. Giving up tea as an economy measure was seriously considered by the family in 1810, soon after they had left Dove Cottage. In the previous year she had settled a tea bill of £13. 14s., perhaps justifying her purchase from London on the grounds of quality, since that same year she had sombrely advised de Quincey to bring tea from London since in the Lake District it was both expensive and of inferior quality. It is typical of the generosity of quite humble folk in the Lakeland of their time that Dorothy can record Molly Fisher inviting them to her home for toast, coffee *and* tea. And the christening of baby John in 1803 was celebrated with a special cake and tea.

Also in this room hang some interesting paintings showing Southey and Coleridge and a fine canvas on loan from the National Portrait Gallery of Thomas Clarkson, a dear friend of the family who devoted his life to the abolition of the slave trade, working closely with Wilberforce, another family friend. A portrait of de Quincey hangs over the fireplace, and his framed marriage certificate, perhaps in silent defiance of the disapproval of his marriage to a local girl, which took place a few months after it properly should have done.

Adjoining this lumber room is a tiny room which visitors might well remember long after all the other rooms have faded in their memory. It was apparently used for a time as a bedroom by Dorothy and at least one if not two of the children simultaneously. Called 'the Newspaper Room', it was lined by Dorothy with copies of the *Morning Chronicle* and *The Times*, which in those days cost 6d. Although the papers were renewed a few years ago, copies from the early years of the nineteenth century were again used. They make fascinating, if eye-watering, reading, for the print is tiny and there seems to have been no illustrated or display advertising in those days. One visitor was so fascinated by this room that he abandoned his family and returned during his holiday to devote a full day to reading them all. When Dorothy papered the room, she could have had no idea of the extent to which present visitors would be fascinated by her primitive interior design. The contents are nothing if not eclectic. Law Reports of cases at the Old Bailey are cheek by jowl with an account of a riot at Farnham; the female fashions for June compete for attention with an announcement of a half guinea reward for the finder of a liver and white spaniel bitch, and we are enjoined to purchase an infallible German cure for corns, bottles of aromatic spirit vinegar and Miller's Welsh Ales. If readers were of an entrepreneurial cast of mind, they might have taken heed of the details of how to apply for a licence to promote a State Lottery.

Dorothy referred to this room as the 'outjutting', and several improvements were effected to make it more convenient, including the raising of the roof and the installation of a new window.

Once the children were fast asleep Dorothy may have breathed a sigh of relief and returned to the fireside to savour the peculiarly refreshing silence that can fall at such moments:

> The Children are now in bed. The evening is very still, and there are no indoor sounds but the ticking of our Family watch which hangs over the chimney-piece . . . and a breathing or a beating of one irregular Flame in my fire. No one who has not been an Inmate with Children in a *Cottage* can have a notion of the quietness that takes possession of it when they are gone to sleep. The hour before is generally a noisy one, often given up to boisterous efforts to amuse them, and the noise is heard in every corner of the house – then comes the washing and undressing, a work of misery, and in ten minutes after, all is stillness and perfect rest. It is at all times a sweet hour to us . . . .

A splendid piece of description from Dorothy which demonstrates, surely, her right to a place alongside the best prose-writers of her time, quite apart from any connection with her famous brother's work. William certainly recognized and acknowledged his sister's genius:

> She gave me eyes, she gave me ears;
> And humble cares, and delicate fears;
> A heart, the fountain of sweet tears;
> And love, and thought, and joy.

A noble and oft quoted acknowledgement. The eminent biographer Robert Gittings suggests that, when William writes of Dorothy giving him eyes and ears, he is perhaps stating an almost literal fact, or at least a fact that is of more than poetic truth. Mr Gittings believes that Dorothy was gifted with long sight and acute hearing and was therefore able to draw attention to many details experienced on, say, a country walk, which William might otherwise miss. This is a most plausible theory when we consider how often in her journals and letters she is capable of the most accurate observations.

To understand fully the Wordsworths' way of life at Town End, it is necessary to inspect not only the inside of the house but also the garden at the front and the 'plot of orchard ground' at the back, this steeply sloping 'nook of mountain ground' which gave them so much pleasure and where Wordsworth often composed his verse. He referred to it as their 'domestic slip of mountain', and it clearly meant a great deal to them, especially after they had built a 'moss hut' at the top of the slope, which commanded even better views of their 'circular vale'.

So frequently did they use the hut that some of their letters are actually addressed and dated 'Moss Hut Wednesday morning' etc. A letter of December 1804 tells of their completing the summer house, 'a little parlour for all of us . . . large enough for a large party to drink tea in . . .'. Dorothy describes it as 'like a wren's nest . . . coated on the outside with heath'. Before this was completed, they also had, lower down the garden, a bower or 'Indian Shed'.

Today the garden is splendidly cared for and is stocked with many of the plants recorded by Dorothy in her Journal. They would often, on their walks, seek out wild flowers, mosses and ferns for transplanting, and once their neighbours learned of their interest, they were given additional specimens. The scarlet runner beans trained up the wall were a source of double pleasure, giving them not only colourful flowers but also an extra variety of vegetable. The vegetable garden proper is now a small lawn, but from many references it is obvious that they were successful in growing an impressive array of food: broccoli, radishes, French beans, peas and cabbages. Less utilitarian plants were also added, and honeysuckle was planted around the yew tree, roses, London pride and apple trees and shrubs. The well too was both a wonderful supply of fresh water and also a source of much delight, and in contrast to the usual image of Wordsworth composing pure and elevated verse as he mused in the garden, there are also references to the need for him to clear out the well and transform it from the 'little muddy pond' it had become.

The idyllic nature of the family's hours spent in the garden is captured by one of the several poems about or addressed to a butterfly:

> This plot of orchard-ground is ours;
> My trees they are, my Sister's flowers; . . .
> Come often to us, fear no wrong;
> Sit near us on the bough!
> We'll talk of sunshine and of song,
> And summer days, when we were young;
> Sweet childish days, that were as long
> As twenty days are now.

Even after the Wordsworths gave up the tenancy of the cottage in May 1808, when they somewhat reluctantly left their 'little nest' where they had become 'crammed . . . edge full', they kept up a close association with it. The new tenant was their friend and admirer Thomas de Quincey, who kept it for almost twenty-eight years, without actually living in it for the whole of his tenancy. The Chairman of the Trustees jokes that, should Wordsworth ever fall from favour, they still have an eminent 'second fiddle' to play in the form of the 'Opium-eater', who in 1818 was joined by his new wife, Peggy Simpson of nearby Nab Farm. Despite his addiction which took place here, he still had many happy experiences and writes lyrically of '. . . the divine pleasures which attend a winter fireside – candles at four o'clock, warm hearth rugs, tea, a fair tea-maker, shutters closed, curtains flowing in ample draperies on the floor, whilst the wind and the rain are raging audibly without . . . .' Possibly the curtains referred to are the very ones which Dorothy had made for him. Though she was less kindly disposed towards him when he later demolished the moss hut and cut down the hedges.

In addition to the row of houses built opposite the cottage after they had left, there was also the building of the Prince of Wales Hotel by the lake shore. In 1830 a certain Mr and Mrs James Flemming were living in a new house at Town End, a year before the present main road was built. It was the Flemmings who, at the Wordsworths' instigation and expense, took in Hartley Coleridge, the wayward son of the poet, agreeing to provide him with lodgings, to mend his stockings and to do his laundry.

Close by the cottage and housed in a cleverly converted coach block is a remarkable museum devoted to 'Grasmere and Wordsworth'. If on arrival the word 'museum' conjures up dusty glass shelves and thorough but boring labels, this idea is quickly dispelled, for here is the fruition of an extraordinary, imaginative and bold idea: to place one of our most famous poets in the context of his time and place. The year the museum was opened, it was given a special award in the Museum of the Year competition. It must have only narrowly missed receiving the highest accolade, for a great deal of painstaking and inspired planning, research, craftsmanship and design have gone into the conversion of the old coach-house and the selection and arrangement of the displays. Local craftsmen have used natural materials of wood and stone to create a fitting setting for the museum's exhibits. These include a highly realistic reconstruction of a farmhouse kitchen. It is night, and the flickering candles reveal a scene with which the Wordsworths were intimately familiar. A few steps further on and the visitor is plummeted dramatically into a well-lit gallery running nearly the full length of the building. Here an array of portraits depicts Wordsworth at different stages of his life and in different moods, and there are portraits of his friends and contemporaries. The Carruthers portrait presides over them all, showing Wordsworth as the grand man in later life, dressed in black with a white frilly dress shirt and his hand on his almost bald head, either in vacant or in pensive mood. When first painted, it was set against the back of the sofa at Rydal Mount, and the reaction of the Wordsworths' servant Betty Youdell from Hacket was, 'God bless us! it comes ower naar.' It is said that when it was first painted Dorothy genuinely mistook the painting for her brother, as she rushed into the room.

A series of panels vividly and economically evoke different stages of Wordsworth's life, including his time at Windebrowe, his period in the West Country, his visits to France and Germany, his life at Rydal Mount, all arranged with a combination of maps, extracts from poems and letters, and explanatory texts. Thus the sense both of people and of place is strong, helped by the humbler everyday objects. The vicious cock spurs, for instance, recall the crueller aspects of the age when cockfights were a popular pastime and the Grasmere area boasted a number of pits. On 6 June 1806 Dorothy records lying awake until one o'clock listening to 'every dog barking cockfighting and other sports'. Happier country traditions are recalled by the lovely Pace or Pasch eggs etched and decorated by the indispensable gardener at Rydal Mount, James Dixon. Queen Victoria received some of his eggs and sent £5 'for the artist'. On Easter Day children would meet to play a kind of 'conker' game with hard-boiled eggs coloured with redwood, alum or onion skins. John West, formerly of Dove Cottage and now custodian of the Hawkshead Grammar School, suggests that the children in Grasmere went from house to house performing a Mummers Play in return for eggs and pennies. The Furness Morris Men have revived these plays, and so once again in parts of Lakeland characters such as Tosspot, Molly Masket, St George and Bessy Brown Bags can be seen.

Anyone wishing to support the work of Dove Cottage is strongly advised to become a 'Friend'. The subscriptions are much needed to continue the impressive work already underway; in return Friends are allowed into the cottage and the museum free of charge, with no limit on the number of visits. Additionally a newsletter is mailed to subscribers which keeps readers up to date with the latest projects and which also contains absorbing and informative articles. Enthusiasm and knowledge are combined in equal quantities. The Chairman of the Trustees, Jonathan

Wordsworth, contributes a regular article on life at Dove
Cottage in a particular year, and the Secretary, Dr Robert
Woof, tells of the latest developments. Individual members of staff give fascinating insights into aspects of their
work, such as the Chief Guide, George Kirkby, telling
some interesting and usually amusing anecdotes.

Mr Kirkby recalls for instance an elderly American
visitor who came one August day in 1977 and declared
that he had last visited the cottage in 1904. He remembered the occasion vividly and recalled his father signing
the visitors' book. George Kirkby thereupon disappeared
behind the scenes and re-emerged with the book for 1904.
Sure enough there was 16 August and the signatures of
the fifty-five visitors who had called that day. And among
them was Dr R. H. Hudnall, with wife and son, from
Blacksburg, Virginia, USA. This set George off on an
investigation of some of the other old visitors' books,
which are now historical documents in their own right.
Place-names such as Constantinople and St Petersburg
are redolent of a distant past, and literary luminaries
are faithfully recorded: A. C. Swinburne, Kate Greena-
way and E. de Selincourt among the regulars. President
Woodrow Wilson paid three separate visits; descendants
of Coleridge, de Quincey and many Wordsworths have left
their names along with Beatrix Potter, Baden Powell and
the Princess of Schleswig-Holstein. George confesses that
his favourite signatures are not so much the famous
names but the ones which set the imagination or the
memory racing: his Aunt Mary who made such mouth-
watering oatcakes, or the signature which reads 'Miss
Lawson & Maid & Coachman' with its evocations of a lost
and leisurely Edwardian age.

George is a fund of anecdotes and has reached the stage
where nothing will surprise him any more, for he has
heard so many unexpected questions: one visitor enquired
whether Walter Scott visited Wordsworth before or after
his expedition to the North Pole, and another, emerging
blinkingly into a sunny day, asked which way he should
now turn to get to Ann Hathaway's Cottage.

One September day the chimney of Wordsworth's bedroom was cleared out, and George sifted through the rubbish 'Klondyke fashion', discovering nothing of great value but plenty of evidence testifying to the collectivitis of generations of jackdaws. Items included a hundredweight of assorted twigs, string, turf, leaves and cowdung; scraps of paper including an advert for ladies shoes costing 7s. 9d a pair; three cigarette packets (Wild Woodbine, Players, Gold Flake); one pipe-cleaner; two feet of fusewire and a lobster claw. No wonder Dorothy complained that the chimney smoked like a furnace. But their next home – Allan Bank – had chimneys which would drive them to distraction, and they would look back on their crowded days at Town End with nostalgia.

2

'The Circular Vale'

The Area around Grasmere

The two houses the Wordsworths occupied after leaving Dove Cottage, namely Allan Bank and The Rectory, are not open to the public, but the scenery surrounding all their former homes is well provided with public ways where we can follow in their footsteps. However, one of the finest Wordsworthian excursions involves not walking but rowing. All members of the family delighted in taking a boat onto Grasmere and landing on the 'solitary green island' in the middle of the lake. On a fine summer day it is an unforgettable experience. Indeed, the island is central to the Wordsworths' lives in both a literal and metaphorical sense, situated in the middle of the lake and enjoying an excellent view of Allan Bank, where Wordsworth spent his middle years.

From the lake are visible other houses with close associations, and which are not easily seen from the land. The long, picturesque façade of the ivy-clad house now called Silver Howe probably occupies the site of 'Gell's Cottage' frequently mentioned in Dorothy's journal and in the letters of several members of the family. When an eccentric bachelor took the cottage, they all watched, with at times delight and at other times anxious concern as the new tenant, Samuel Barber, 'a dashing man from Manchester', began to develop and change the house and grounds. It was owned by the archaeologist William (later Sir William) Gell, who, despite his calling, seems to have raised no objection to the changes wrought by Barber. Writing in 1822, Mary states that the property 'is looking at its very best', but when Barber first took the cottage around 1805, they feared his ideas would prove too 'fantastical' for their tastes. He also took the island at the same time, and there was much apprehension about his plans to erect some monstrous obelisk, thus spoiling one of their favourite spots. During Gell's residence they frequently borrowed his boat for fishing expeditions, which, in the manner of such things, at times enjoyed conspicuous success, and at others failed miserably. Dorothy has references to William and their brother John catching on one occasion fourteen bass, and on another two pike at the Loughrigg end of the lake. They baked the fish, which they seemed to consider a great treat – with no mention of the countless tiny bones which deter most of us from persisting with this particular fish.

Ideally one should take a picnic here in the style of the Wordsworths. Dorothy on one visit looks nostalgically at the charred stones on the island, a reminder of a happy meal there one summer – they took a kettle and used water from the lake. At this period the idea of a picnic was something new – an import from the Continent, and Dorothy speculates on the origin and derivation of the word, which she takes to be German. The new fashion certainly caught on with them, and a good number of the giblet pies and gooseberry tarts she records baking must have been consumed on the island. Prints and paintings of the time suggest that the island was not as well wooded as it is today, but even then sheep were grazed on its rich pastures. Dorothy refers to an occasion when their intent to visit the island was abandoned because of a thunderstorm, and she rejoices in their disappointment as she was reluctant to disturb the sheep grazing so peacefully. The stone outhouse was certainly there – it features in paintings of the time, and Wordsworth wrote some verses on a stone in the wall of the barn:

> Thou see'st a homely Pile, yet to these walls
> The heifer comes in the snow-storm, and here

The new-dropped lamb finds shelter from the wind
And hither does one Poet sometimes row
His pinnace, a small vagrant barge, up-piled
With plenteous store of heath and withered fern . . .
Spreads out his limbs, while, yet unshorn, the Sheep,
Panting beneath the burthen of their wool,
Lie round him, even as if they were a part
Of his own household: nor, while from his bed
He looks, through the open door-place, toward the lake
And to the stirring breezes, does he want
Creations lovely as the work of sleep –
Fair sights, and visions of romantic joy.

'A temple of abomination' was how Wordsworth described Allan Bank when it was built by a Liverpool couple, Mr and Mrs Crump. Certainly the house does still dominate many views of the vale of Grasmere. Though his assertion that the building destroys the character and simplicity of its surroundings is a matter of opinion. By June 1808 he had either changed his opinion or was prepared to swallow his pride, for it was then that Allan Bank became his family's home. True they had little choice of rented properties in the area suitable for their growing family, and in their final years at Dove Cottage they had often considered the desirability of moving house. Indeed, they were determined that any house they rented subsequent to Dove Cottage would be on a yearly basis in case they decided to leave the area completely and settle in the warmer, drier area of Kent or eastern England.

But any anxieties they might have had must have quickly dissolved on arriving at their new home in what is usually the most glorious month of the Lakeland year. Although Allan Bank is not open to the public, a footpath runs close to one side of the house which gives an excellent idea of the feature that made the property so desirable – the astonishing panorama to be enjoyed from this vantage-point overlooking the vale of Grasmere. To walk this path, one begins in the main square of the village; a lane marked 'no through road' goes off from one corner of the square (with the Red Lion to the left, and to the right the coffee shop and bank), and this leads past Allan Bank, which is on the left as one follows the pleasant lane onto Scaur Fell. The sense almost of parkland here is not an illusion: Wordsworth gained the Crumps' permission to plant trees in the surrounding grounds a full year before he moved in, suggesting that he was to make this a permanent home after all. Presumably many of the trees we admire today were the result of this foresight. Perhaps it also helped to placate his pride, considering his earlier strictures about the house intruding into the valley.

De Quincey asserts that the very building of the house was by no means uneventful. Mr Crump, distrustful of the abilities of local builders was unwise enough to bring up his own workmen from Liverpool. It was a mistake he was to regret bitterly, for de Quincey records with some glee how the workmen, on completing the erection of the walls of the house, repaired to the Red Lion to celebrate their progress. But pride cometh before a fall. Even as they were 'carousing', a traveller rode up to the inn '. . . who brought them the unseasonable news, that, whilst riding along the vale, he had beheld the downfall of the whole building. Out the men rushed, hoping this might be a hoax; but too surely they found his report true, and their own festival premature.' Not surprisingly, de Quincey describes the 'little malice mingled with laughter' of the local builders who had been snubbed in favour of the demonstrably incompetent team from the city.

The patience and health of the Wordsworths were to be sorely tried as a result of the house's structural faults, but these were not yet apparent to Dorothy when she arrived in splendid weather to savour the extensive views the site commanded of Seat Sandal and Fairfield 'now green to their very summits'. And not only were there elevated views to admire after their years at lake-level for the adults now also had the luxury of separate rooms in a house spacious enough to ensure that the noises of the children at play did not penetrate every corner of the house. Soon de Quincey was staying for many months and there were visits from Coleridge, whose children Hartley

and Derwent regularly spent two days a week at Allan
Bank from their school lodgings in Ambleside. Often there
could be as many as fifteen people under Allan Bank's roof,
and the temptation to escape to the wild solitude of the fell
above the house must frequently have been great.

Dorothy's ecstasy on arrival was short-lived. The house
which was so idyllic in the heat of summer proved to be a
nightmare when the gales of autumn and the snows of
winter arrived. The Wordsworths had persistent trouble
at Allan Bank with 'smoky chimneys' despite constant
efforts by builders, who at one stage actually demolished
and reconstructed a whole chimneypiece. It became so bad
that only one room – William's study – was relatively
unaffected, and here they were obliged to retreat to be
warm, and also to cook their food. On at least one occasion
– and this at midday – the smoke was so thick that they
could not see each other in the same room. The children
complained of sore and red eyes, and a thick layer of soot
covered everything.

They occupied Allan Bank for almost three years, from
June 1808 to May 1811. Willy, the youngest child, was
born there on 12 May 1810. Six weeks later William and
Dorothy left Mary with her children at Allan Bank while
they embarked on a tour which included a visit to Sir
George Beaumont's home in Leicestershire.

During this absence William and Mary exchanged letters which have only recently come to light, and in quite
extraordinary circumstances. They first came to the notice
of the public in a sale at Sotheby's, the London auc-
tioneers. The successful bid came from an American University, Cornell, the home both of some noted Wordsworth
scholars and of some fine paintings and manuscripts; they
paid £38,500 for the William–Mary correspondence, at the
time the property of a young Carlisle stamp-dealer who
had found them among a bundle for which he had paid the
princely sum of £5. The stamp-dealer was accustomed to
advertise in local papers for old letters, and tinkers would
often bring him bundles from demolition sites for which he
usually paid £5. But this particular batch on closer inspection proved disappointing; it appeared that the papers had

already been sifted for postmarks and stamps. But as he was about to consign them to the incinerator, he noticed the name Wordsworth, which alerted him to their possible value; thus came about their ultimate appearance in Sotheby's catalogue. Cornell generously sold them to the Dove Cottage Trustees for the same price they had paid at the auction, and they are now 'back home' at Grasmere, cared for by the Dove Cottage Library and published in several handsome volumes of varying prices. Royalties from the book sales benefit Dove Cottage.

The Wordsworths' next home was the Grasmere Rectory. Though they had arrived there in May 1811 with high hopes of happiness after the discomforts of Allan Bank, their two-year stay was almost entirely clouded by the tragedy of Catherine's and Thomas's death. However, there was at least one jolly Christmas when they feasted off their traditional yuletide fare of Roast Beef and Plum Pudding – only the use of capitals can convey the delight such traditions gave to Dorothy, celebrating her birthday and Christmas. Indeed during the years at Dove Cottage, Christmas week was triply celebrated as the time of the year when they first set up home again in the Lake District.

Little asides in the letters of this period show many moments of domestic bliss before tragedy hit the family: dancing in the kitchen to the tunes of a vigorously played fiddle; the arrival of a pig and the children's joy on learning that it was to be kept to produce piglets; the charming description by Dorothy of the carefree John jauntily walking each day to his school in Ambleside '. . . with a Tin Bottle on his shoulder and a Basket on his arm'. Dorothy too enjoyed her walks and even in her fortieth year boasted of leaving the Rectory for daily walks of up to twenty miles on occasions, with lengths of ten and twelve miles by no means uncommon.

At this house Wordsworth continued work on 'The Excursion', but his most memorable poem written in the gloomy study of the house inevitably recalls the deaths of his children:

Surprised by joy – impatient as the wind
I turned to share the transport – Oh with whom
But thee, deep buried in the silent tomb,
That spot which no vicissitude can find?
Love, faithful love, recalled thee to my mind –
But how could I forget thee? Through what power
Even for the least division of an hour,
Have I been so beguiled as to be blind
To my most grievous loss – That thought's return
Was the worst pang that sorrow ever bore,
Save one, one only, when I stood forlorn,
Knowing my heart's best treasure was no more;
That neither present time, nor years unborn
Could to my sight that heavenly face restore.

As always happens on such occasions, the deaths brought a close family even closer together, and a new determination enters their letters to distant friends and relatives urging them to visit the Lakes or hoping that they might embark on journeys to other parts of the country. The schooling of the surviving children begins to concern them more, and the help of de Quincey (now settled at Dove Cottage) is enlisted to teach the ten-year-old John to read Latin. De Quincey boasted that, with only an hour's tuition each day for six weeks, he could teach even an average scholar to understand the language. Dorothy, herself no mean teacher, takes waspish delight in recording the failure of this unrealistic plan: 'The said nominal hour is now included in the space of twenty minutes; either the scholar learns with such uncommon rapidity that more is unnecessary, or the master tires. Which of these conjectures is the more probable I leave you to guess.'

By the side of the church that fronts the Rectory, is a good view from the elevated churchyard of a row of cottages known as Church Stile. At one end of the row is a tiny National Trust Information Centre where helpful attendants are rarely at a loss to answer visitors' enquiries – the Trust owning and protecting a great deal of property in the Grasmere area. At the other end of the row is a discreet artist's studio. These cottages are frequently mentioned as being in Wordsworth's day the village inn owned and run by Robert Newton. It was in these cottages that friends of the family – the Clarksons – once stayed, and on subsequent visits to the churchyard Dorothy always remembered with pleasure Mrs Clarkson's rooms with the windows half open and the white curtains. If this picturesque row did not have to 'compete' with more famous houses in the area, it would no doubt command the scrutiny of many literary pilgrims, for the associations are rich and varied. As an inn it had the honour of hosting Samuel Taylor Coleridge and Wordsworth during their walking tour of the Lakes in 1799. Many years later it was to provide a congenial home for the wayward but likeable son of Coleridge, Hartley, whose erratic behaviour and addiction to alcoholic beverages was to cause his friends much anxiety. In 1810 Dorothy writes to Lady Beaumont, giving her details of Newton's alterations to the property, when he raised the roof at one end and added another sash window, features which can still be seen.

Further along the village street, the Red Lion is still a busy inn serving the needs of both local residents and visitors. Hartley Coleridge was also an habitué of this hostelry, whose landlord, Jonathan Bell, drowned himself in the lake in 1830. So much time did Hartley spend in the company of this man that Wordsworth used to refer good-humouredly to him as 'Mr Bell's scholar'.

The road past the Red Lion goes for a few hundred yards to a spot which was much loved by all the Wordsworths and whose beauty is now protected forever by the National Trust. This is Butharlyp How, a wooded knoll opposite the Rothay Bank Hotel. A footpath goes through a gate and quickly turns away from the traffic into a leafy retreat. De Quincey used to indulge a fancy that he would one day buy it as a birthday gift for little Dora Wordsworth. When the land was advertised for sale in 1810, Mary Wordsworth urged him seriously to consider buying the property, if only to prevent it from falling into the hands of the dreaded Astley family from Manchester whose unruly behaviour drew much 'tut-tutting' from locals at the time.

There are many references in Dorothy's journal to 'Butterlip How' as she called it, and it was clearly a favourite destination for short walks in all weathers. There are descriptions of the views from the hill in sunshine and rain, frost and snow, and even a description of a jaunt there under the light of the moon, when the vale 'looked spacious and very beautiful – the level meadows seemed very large, and some nearer us unequal ground heaving like sand'. On another occasion a combination of Dorothy's aversion to cattle and a very boggy field forced her and William to curtail a longer excursion and instead walk backwards and forwards by Butharlyp: 'Every horned cow puts me in terror . . . walked backwards and forwards between Goody Bridge and Butterlip How.'

One can still today enjoy the level walk with its views towards Helm Crag, Dunmail and Seat Sandal, a view even more enjoyable from the tiny tree-topped summit of the 'how' itself. The path passes through another gate, which gives access to the Easedale road. Here one may either retrace steps or turn left along the road back into the village. When Prince Leopold passed through the Lakes in 1817, Wordsworth specifically recommended the royal visitor to walk on Butharlyp – and this some four years after leaving the immediate Grasmere area. He clearly continued to place this spot high on his list of 'musts'.

But the greatest 'must' for visitors to Grasmere is back in the very centre of the village: St Oswald's Church, which during the Wordsworths' occupation of Dove Cottage was experiencing an unfortunate period in its history. The rector who died in 1806 had never lived in the rectory and seems to have been insane for most if not all of the astonishingly long period (sixty-three years) in which he held his office. The curate in charge at this time seems not to have inspired his flock either by word or by deed. Dorothy in her journal for 3 September 1800 describes a funeral she attended at the house of John Dawson, one of their neighbours who lived at How Top between Dove Cottage and White Moss Common. She was in tearful mood as she joined the funeral procession down to the

church and must have been deeply distressed by the
lamentable reception the curate gave them:

> The green fields, neighbours of the churchyard, were as green
> as possible and with the brightness of the sunshine looked
> quite gay . . . I could not help weeping very much. When we
> came to the bridge they began to sing again and stopped
> during four lines before they entered the churchyard. The
> priest met us – he did not look as a man ought to do on such an
> occasion – I had seen him half drunk the day before in a
> pot-house. Before we came with the corpse one of the company
> observed he wondered what sort of cue 'our parson would be
> in.'

This curate was the deservedly notorious Edward Row-
landson, and when Dorothy (as she surely must) reported
the incident to her brother, he must have shared her grief,
for in Book II of 'The Excursion' he shows in verse that
same sensitivity to death revealed by Dorothy in her
prose:

> . . . What traveller . . . does not own
> The bond of brotherhood, when he sees them go,
> A mute procession on the houseless road . . .
> . . . when the body, soon to be consigned
> Ashes to ashes, dust bequeathed to dust,
> Is raised from the church-aisle, and forward borne
> Upon the shoulders of the next in love. . . .

Perhaps this parlous state of St Oswald's Church
accounts for the fact that the Wordsworths seem not to
have been regular worshippers there during this period.
Today the church impresses by its unusual beauty and by
the sense of piety evoked by an ancient building occupying
a site where God has been worshipped since Saxon times.
The most immediately striking feature is the actual construction. Rough-hewn whitewashed walls and pillars of
substantial girth testify to the material origins of this
unique building, namely massive boulders from the nearby River Rothay bound together by strong mortar. The
walls and pillars are decorated largely by brown var-

nishcd boards lettered in gold with short Biblical texts.
Bearing in mind the character of both the rector and his
wayward curate, these injunctions to leading a Christian
life might have rung somewhat hollow in the ears of the
more pious worshippers. Job, the Psalms and Proverbs
seem to have been favourite sources. But if Wordsworth
and his tolerably law-abiding contemporaries of the parish needed no such commandments to dissuade them from
murder and adultery, they might nonetheless have found
the text on one board at least to their liking: 'The rich and
poor meet together. The Lord is the Maker of them all. . . .
Give me neither poverty nor riches. Feed me food convenient for me.'

These homely homilies on their rough boards provide a
curiously pleasing contrast with the other tablets which
adorn the white walls. Most of these are of more recent
date and of marble. The most notable is the handsome
marble memorial to Wordsworth placed high on the wall
to the left of and at right angles to the altar. The description and dedication – elevated both literally and stylisti-
cally – were penned by the eminent Oxford theologian
John Keble:

TO THE MEMORY OF
WILLIAM WORDSWORTH
A TRUE PHILOSOPHER AND POET
WHO BY THE SPECIAL GIFT AND CALLING OF
ALMIGHTY GOD
WHETHER HE DISCOURSED ON MAN OR NATURE
FAILED NOT TO LIFT UP THE HEART
TO HOLY THINGS
TIRED NOT OF MAINTAINING THE CAUSE
OF THE POOR AND SIMPLE;
AND SO IN PERILOUS TIMES WAS RAISED UP
TO BE A CHIEF MINISTER
NOT ONLY OF NOBLEST POESY
BUT OF HIGH AND SACRED TRUTH.
THIS MEMORIAL
IS PLACED HERE BY HIS FRIENDS AND NEIGHBOURS
IN TESTIMONY OF
RESPECT AFFECTION AND GRATITUDE.

At the top of the oblong tablet is a wreath of laurel leaves, and below the inscription, in bas-relief, a profile of the poet showing the high forehead and prominent nose which feature in so many portraits of him made at various stages in his long life. Above the memorial and slightly to the left, balanced on the ledge of one of the wall arcades, is an impish, gargoyle-like head which was discovered during building work on the church. Presumably it was placed there by a verger in a wry mood, knowing that visitors paying homage at the memorial might be struck by the contrast between the elegantly carved profile of the Poet Laureate and the elvish grimace of the carved head.

From this same position, but glancing to the right, can be seen another carving, placed close to the altar, supported by a small oak ledge. This carved stone is thought to be a portion of a cross shaft, possibly twelfth century, decorated on all four sides. The piscina in the south wall has been re-dressed and moved to its present position. Admire too the splendidly carved chairs close to the altar, reminiscent of the remarkable oak carved furniture to be seen at Town End Farmhouse at Troutbeck. The Bishop's chair is inscribed 'T.L. 1677', and the other chair bears the initials 'M.B. 1703'. If one looks up and back along the nave, traces of the roof of an earlier building are visible in the notches in the rafters which carried the supporting spars. Similar notches have been discovered under the rough cast of the tower. This marvellous combination of exposed rafters with the great bulk and strength of the pillars produces a most striking effect, characterized by Wordsworth's economical lines:

Not raised in nice proportions was the pile,
But large and massy; for duration built;
With pillars crowded, and the roof upheld
By naked rafters intricately crossed . . .
Like leafless underboughs, in some thick wood. . . .

The northern aisle was added at a later date, probably in the sixteenth century, and it was then that the old (northern) wall was pierced at intervals to connect with the 'new extension', still referred to as the 'Langdale aisle'. It is this unusual solution to the problem of enlarging the church which accounts for its unique interior, for the north aisle and the nave originally had separate roofs. Later they were combined and a second tier of arches was built upon the lower tier of the central wall to support it. Note how the columns of the upper arches rest upon the crowns of the lower. The aisle is a yard narrower than the nave, and outside it is apparent that the roof had to be elbowed, causing a break in the lines. No wonder Grasmere can boast a church which is totally unlike any other when we consider how the ingenious local builders have wrestled over the centuries with their various problems and unique solutions. Wordsworth catches the atmosphere beautifully and aptly when he refers to the building's 'rude and antique majesty'.

The church's present floor of local flagstones was formerly strewn with an equally local, if less durable, covering, namely rushes. This tradition lives on in the annual Rushbearing Ceremony, held each year on the Saturday nearest to St Oswald's Day. This charming festival begins at 4.30 p.m. precisely, when splendid garlands and baskets of flowers, rushes and heathers are brought by village children to the churchyard wall. Each child is given a new penny, and the bearers then process around the village in the company of the clergy and choir. The rushmaidens dressed specially for the ceremony in picturesque and identical style, carrying their sheet by the sides and corners like a gigantic handkerchief, while held proudly aloft is the wavering embroidered banner of St Oswald. With such richly decorated finery, they must be thankful that the saint's day falls on 5 August when there is at least some expectation of fine weather. The local newspapers usually send a photographer to cover the event, and an investigation of their archives will reveal how undaunted the local children are by the vagaries of the Lakeland weather. Perhaps they are fortified by the gift they know awaits them at the end of the ceremony, for what child could resist a specially baked piece of that celebrated sweetmeat, Grasmere gingerbread, especially when, as on this occasion, it is stamped with the name of St Oswald. In former times adults took part, and their reward was strong ale. Indeed the day became an excuse to pay homage to Bacchus rather than Oswald. The 'simple water-drinking bard' would approve of the present decorous pageant, and his vivid vignette of this 'rural ceremony' is worth recalling:

> The village children, while the sky is red
> With evening lights, advance in long array
> Through the still churchyard, each with garland gay,
> That, carried sceptre-like, o'ertops the head
> Of the proud bearer. To the wide church door,
> Charged with these offerings which their fathers bore
> For decoration in the Papal time,
> The innocent procession softly moves . . . .

In former times each door of the church was used by the three different 'townships' which made up the parish, Grasmere itself, Langdale and finally Rydal, Loughrigg and that portion of Ambleside known as 'Above Stock(beck)'. The south gate was used by these latter parishioners; the west gate was used by the Langdalians; and the north or lych gate was used by the Grasmerians.

The gingerbread shop by the lych gate still sells the 'Celebrated Sarah Nelson's Gingerbread', made to a secret recipe; the bread is not, as you might expect, soft, but a hard slab wrapped in waxed paper; it is mouth-watering and literally melts on the tongue.

During Wordsworth's lifetime this gingerbread shop was the local schoolhouse. He and his family always took a great interest in education and indeed came to know intimately some of the greatest educators of the Victorian age; several became close neighbours in his later years, such as Dr Thomas and Matthew Arnold. One eminent educationist, Dr Andrew Bell, who advocated the controversial 'Madras' system, condescended to allow Wordsworth to show him the village school during a brief visit in 1811. Bell advocated the use of 'pupil teachers' as a means

Grasmere: lake and island from Red Bank, with Dunmail Raise in the background

Grasmere: St. Oswald's Church (*right*); Rectory (*below right*)

Grasmere: Dove Cottage (*left*); Allan Bank (*below*)

Rydal Mount (*above left*)

Wordsworth's Summerhouse, Rydal Mount (*left*)

Rydalwater from Rydal Mount

Ann Tyson's
Cottage,
Hawkshead

Ann Tyson's Cottage,
Green End Cottage,
Colthouse

Hawkshead School

Esthwaitewater

Ferry Landing, Windermere
(*above*)

Wordsworth Court, Bowness

of educating large numbers of children, and Wordsworth's enthusiasm for the system led him to teach regularly in the school for two or three hours each day that autumn. But, to borrow Gibbon's phrase, other avocations intervened, and he was content to leave further teaching to his sister Dorothy, his wife Mary and Mary's sister Sara Hutchinson, all of whose remains are now buried in the churchyard.

In St Oswald's Churchyard there is a headstone that leads so many people astray

WILLIAM WORDSWORTH
1883
FANNY WORDSWORTH
1888

Who was Fanny? people ask, and surely William did not live to be 113 years old? The mystery is quickly solved: William's youngest son shared the same name (he was known as Willy to distinguish him from his father). He married Fanny Graham, who outlived him by some five years, dying in 1888. It is their tombstone which causes so much confusion. To the right of this stone another, equally simple slab marks the spot where Dorothy was laid to rest in 1855. Then to the left of this is not a gravestone as one might think but a memorial to Dorothy's and William's dear brother:

IN MEMORY OF
JOHN WORDSWORTH
BROTHER OF WILLIAM AND DOROTHY
A SILENT POET CHERISHED VISITANT
AND LOVER OF THIS VALLEY. BORN 4 DEC
1772 HE DIED AT HIS POST AS COMMANDER
OF THE EARL OF ABBERGAVENNY WHICH
WAS WRECKED IN THE ENGLISH CHANNEL
5th FEBRUARY 1805. HE WAS BURIED AT
WYKE REGIS

Immediately below the memorial to John Wordsworth is an inscribed stone:

Here lies the body/of/Sarah Hutchinson, beloved Sister & faithful friend of Mourners who have caused this stone to be erected / with an earnest wish that their own remains / may be laid by her side and an humble hope / that, through Christ, they may together be Made partakers of the same blessed resurrection. She was born at Penrith 1st January 1775 / and died at Rydal 23rd June 1835 / In fulfilment of that wish / Are now gathered near her the remains of / William Wordsworth, born at Cockermouth 7th April 1770, died at Rydal 23rd April 1850 / and of Dorothy Wordsworth / born at Cockermouth 25th December 1771, / died at Rydal 25th January 1855; / and finally, of Mary Wordsworth, / wife of William Wordsworth, / and sister of Sarah Hutchinson; / Born at Penrith August 16th 1770; / died at Rydal Mount 17th January 1859.

The saddest stones are the ones of young Catherine and Thomas, victims, as so many youngsters of that age were, of a combination of illnesses, including measles and pneumonia.

Not that these stones are the sole reminders of the family. Close by is a yew tree, one of eight churchyard yews planted by William, who in Book VII of 'The Excursion' penned lines which may be appropriate for the graves of his own family:

> 'These grassy heaps lie amicably close,'
> Said I, 'like surges heaving in the wind
> Along the surface of a mountain pool. . . .'

Nearer the church are buried members of another local family, the Greens, victims of a tragedy which moved the whole parish to tears and to action when it occurred in 1808. According to Dorothy's account, George Green and his wife had been to Langdale one cold morning to attend a sale. As they returned over the tops to their cottage in Easedale, they seem to have been overtaken by the adverse weather conditions. Back home seven children were awaiting their return. Sally, the eldest child, sat up late that Saturday night before concluding that her parents must have stayed over in Langdale. When they still had not returned on the Monday, she went to a neighbour to borrow a cloak that she might search for them. When the neighbour heard her story, he immediately raised the alarm, and some sixty folk turned out to search the fells. But all in vain. The Greens had perished in the snow, and the children were left orphaned. A fund was set up which quickly attracted some £600, and the orphans were taken care of by a grief-stricken parish. Dorothy supervised the adoptions of the children and has left a most moving account of the reception each child received at the several foster homes.

The death of their two children at the Rectory made a move inevitable. Not only did the house harbour unbearable memories of their deaths, it also looked out onto their very graves. The churchyard which had formerly rung to their happy cries was now a constant reminder of their deaths. It is impossible to look up at the bedrooms of the Rectory today without recalling the anguish the family must have suffered. Dorothy wrote to de Quincey about Catherine's death in June 1812 when both William and Mary were away in different parts of the country: 'I am grieved at heart . . . but you must bear the sad tidings – our sweet little Catherine was seized with convulsions on Wednesday night . . . the fits continued till ¼ after five in the morning, when she breathed her last. . . . She never forgot Quincey – dear Innocent she now lies upon her Mother's Bed, a perfect image of peace. . . .' When Thomas died in December, it was Dorothy who was away from their Rectory home, and it was William who had to break the news to de Quincey, always a great favourite with the children.

Not surprisingly they left the Rectory the following year to settle at Rydal Mount. Dorothy was the last to leave the house, quitting on May Day 1813:

The weather is delightful, and the place a paradise: but my inner thoughts *will* go back to Grasmere. I was the last person who left the house yesterday evening. It seemed as quiet as the grave; and the very churchyard where our darlings lie, when I gave a last look upon it [seemed] to chear [*sic*] my thoughts. There I could think of life and immortality – the house only reminded me of desolation, gloom, emptiness and the chearless silence – but why do I now turn to these thoughts? the morning is bright and I am more chearful today.

3

The Rydal Round

The House and Grounds of Rydal Mount

Inevitably Rydal is associated with the Wordsworths' later lives. After all, William did live at Rydal Mount for thirty-seven years, Dorothy for forty-two years, and Mary for forty-six years. All three died at the Mount. Yet their associations with this area go back long before they moved into Rydal Mount in 1813. It was at Rydal in 1800 that Dorothy resolved to keep her immortal *Grasmere Journals*. She had just said farewell to brothers William and John, who were on their way to visit William's future wife, their childhood friend Mary Hutchinson, then staying near Scarborough. It was 14 May, and she was returning from Low Wood, whence she had accompanied them. Her heart, she writes, was made easier after a flood of tears. At Pelter Bridge, by the road at the foot of the steep lane leading up to Rydal Mount, she paused to admire the view, and '. . . resolved to write a journal of the time till W. and J. return . . . and because I shall give Wm Pleasure by it when he comes home again . . .'.

As she walked along, she stopped often and sat down, noticing with her keen eye for such things many details of the countryside, and, as she looked up to the head of Rydal, admiring many 'sweet views . . . when I could juggle away the fine houses, but they disturbed me . . .'. Thirteen years later she was living in one of those fine houses. In the following years she often refers to walks in this area, mentioning the excursions from Dove Cottage to admire

53

the views from the road to Rydal. In 1804 she records William's particular excitement at discovering, 'near the famous waterfalls', an old kite's nest in a secluded section of the stream above the falls. The strangely shaped oaks and birches and the tumbling stream greatly affected them, and they felt they had made a real discovery.

The waterfalls at Rydal were a major attraction for Lake District tourists of that time. It was as compulsory for a Lakeland visitor to view the falls of Rydal as it is today for a visitor to Paris to see the Eiffel Tower. They were very frequently painted by both amateur and profess-ional alike. A particularly fine study was executed by the famous Wright of Derby, and for many years there was a 'summer house' carefully positioned so that the 'correct' view was framed by an open window. Here artists could contentedly sketch, protected from the weather. Although these falls are easily accessible today, they are often left out of the most comprehensive guidebooks and even omit-ted from pamphlets which specifically recommend water-falls.

When the Dowager Queen Adelaide visited Words-worth in August 1840, she was conducted by the poet to the falls as her very first 'treat' on arriving at Rydal. He and Coleridge, on their walking tour of 1799, spent two nights at Robert Newton's inn at Grasmere, from where they went one evening to Rydal specifically to see the falls. They saw them, according to Wordsworth 'through the gloom, and it was very magnificent'. Coleridge was ec-static: 'I cannot express for myself how deeply I have been impressed by a world of scenery absolutely new to me. At Rydal & Grasmere I recd [received] I think the deepest delight. . . .' On another occasion Wordsworth compared Lakeland's waterfalls very favourably with those of Switzerland, making it clear that the Rydal Falls were very familiar to him: 'The natural imagery of these views was supplied by frequent, I might say intense, observation of the Rydal Torrent. What an animating contrast is the ever-changing of that, and indeed of every one of our mountain brooks, to the monotonous tone and unmiti-gated fury of such streams among the Alps. . . .' In 1819

Wordsworth wrote to Lord Lonsdale suggesting that, among the sights his Lordship should show his guest, Prince Leopold, were '. . . the grounds of Rydal Hall with their Waterfalls . . . known to everyone'.

William's *Guide* seems at variance with Dorothy's references to Rydal before they came to live there, for he specifically mentions that, 'Rydalmere is nowhere seen to advantage from the *main road*. Fine views may be had from Rydal Park; but these grounds, as well as those of Rydal Mount . . . are private.' In fact, once they were ensconced at the Mount, they had the double bonus of access to the grounds there and to those of Rydal Park, for in 1815 Lord and Lady Beaumont were staying at the Mount for, according to Dorothy, 'nine delightful summer days . . . wandering all the mornings in the park, which is as good as our own'.

Visitors staying in Ambleside can forsake their cars and walk through the park along a fine right of way which begins just outside the town through some imposing iron gates and continues to the right of Rydal Hall itself and behind the main building, now a diocesan Conference Centre. This conveniently comes out close to the entrance of Rydal Mount. After visiting the house and falls, the visitor can continue to Dove Cottage along a route which Wordsworth recommends in his *Guide*: 'A foot road passing behind Rydal Mount and under Nab Scar to Grasmere, is very favourable to views of the Lake and the Vale, looking back towards Ambleside.'

If this route is followed, cast an eye on the slopes above and think of the scene described by Wordsworth in a letter written in June 1829: 'You would have enjoyed a walk I had this morning with Miss Coleridge now our visitor. With a spade, each a basket and an umbrella, for sunny showers were flying all about us – we went high up in a valley among the mountains behind this house to fetch the roots of a beautiful flower which she had seen for the first time a few days ago. We have planted it in the garden with many fears however that the soil is not moist enough for it to thrive in.' This practice of transplanting wild flowers is now much frowned upon by naturalists and conservationists; strictures against it are enshrined in the Country Code, and it is even illegal under many circumstances.

A visit to Rydal Mount must rank as one of the high spots of any Wordsworthian pilgrimage. Both house and gardens are beyond praise. Mary (née Wordsworth) Henderson, a great-great-granddaughter of William, took the bold and imaginative step of acquiring the property and opening it to the public. Generous donations of authentic furniture and memorabilia were made, and over the years more items have been added to the collection. Open seven days a week for most of the year, it is sensitively cared for by dedicated guides and custodians.

The first room belongs to the oldest part of the house, which dates back to the mid-sixteenth century. It is on the right of the entrance corridor and is known as the dining-room. There are striking features which would make the room of interest even if it had no connection with the Wordsworths. The spice cupboard in the far corner, built into the wall just to the left of the firegrate, is a feature of the farmhouses of Westmorland. In this cupboard, which recedes deeply into the wall, the salt and other culinary spices could be kept dry. These were of course treasured condiments in the days before freezers kept food 'fresh' regardless of the seasons. The small door to the cupboard is flush with the wall and is carved with the date 1710. The locks recall how precious spices were once considered. The custodians have placed an array of them in the cupboard, which, an opening, brings a mixture of aromas: chilli, cloves, cinnamon and coriander. The initials 'E A K' on the carved door recall that Edward and Agnes Knott owned the house from 1700 to 1750.

The parish register records that in 1574 the house was a small yeoman-style cottage, and in the early days the entrance was by the alcove in this room. The thick wall of the passage was then the outside wall of the much smaller original cottage, which in the mid-eighteenth century was transformed into a much more substantial dwelling by the addition of the drawing-room wing. When Ford North bought it in 1803 for £2,500, he renamed it Rydal Mount. It was sold to Lady Flemming of nearby Rydal Hall in

1812, the year before Wordsworth rented it from her ladyship.

Other items in the room of special interest include the copy of the Haydon portrait made when Wordsworth was forty-eight years old. Mary greatly admired it but Dorothy was less enthusiastic. The original is owned by the National Portrait Gallery, but in their day it hung in this room. The painter said that many people had considered this drawing to be 'the best sketch I had ever made of anyone . . .'. Wordsworth wrote to the artist that, although some found it a 'stodgy' likeness, he himself '. . . was proud to possess it as a mark of your regard, and for its own merits'.

The dining-table chairs have been in the Wordsworth family since the Rydal Mount days and so, like the copy portrait, have a double claim to their place here. But tables, chairs and crockery, however accurate, cannot fully convey the history of this room in which countless meals must have been consumed by the family and their many and often distinguished guests. To reconstruct the menus of their time their letters must be scoured for occasional references; these can be few and far between, but slowly, as one reads through them, a most interesting reconstruction can be made of the kind of meals they must have enjoyed in this room.

Some furnishings and artefacts have already given clues to the family's eating habits: the spice cupboard; the grand tea-caddy at Dove Cottage; Wordsworth's picnic box displayed in the glass-cabinet in the library drawing-room. Other indications are rarer and less tangible. Often they are asides in letters about the weather, or thank-you notes for food gifts received from friends, or remarks about the vegetable garden; 1816, for instance, was a poor year for honey; presumably, therefore, other years were better, and honey was often part of their diet. Cowslip wine was apparently a special treat, for Dorothy records drinking some on 25 December – her birthday as well as the day of more general celebration. In the same year that the honey was poor, the gooseberries were not doing too well either. When brother Richard, the lawyer, died, William writes to the Penrith solicitor responsible for looking after Richard's local affairs to say that '. . . as I am in want of wine myself. . . [I] will take it at valuation', referring to the contents of his brother's wine cellar at Sockbridge. He must have enjoyed drinking that wine much more than his remedy for nausea: 'cold camomile tea with a little brandy'. His restorative for general debilitation sounds preferable, consisting of port wine heated in a hot pan with cinnamon and cloves (presumably kept at hand in the spice cupboard). Perhaps this was a remedy that became too expensive, for in 1833 he is writing emphatically to a friend, 'We must not think of purchasing more Port wine till the price falls.' Perhaps in a similar mood of economy they brewed their own ale. Dorothy seems to have been particularly adventurous, taking a pinch of snuff and sampling oysters. She is effusive over many food gifts, including the '. . . long black skinned potatoes – the best in the world . . .', the venison and partridges sent by Lord Lowther, the 'pannier of beautiful apples', the 'excellent haddock' and the fine 'mountain mutton and Westmorland beef' which the Wilberforce family consumed on one of their visits.

The original fireplace was in the opposite wall from the present fireplace, clearly discernible by the large alcove which now contains a china display. The 'new' firegrate is the one the Wordsworths knew, the blue Delft tiles having been given by their friend Henry Crabb Robinson.

A sketch by Haydon of Wellington and his horse at Waterloo is inscribed 'B R Haydon to William Wordsworth 1840 with affection and gratitude'. Close by is the sonnet which this drawing inspired and which begins:

By Art's bold privilege Warrior and Warhorse stand
On ground yet strewn with their last battle's wreck. . . .

On a wooden wine-table is an old lock and key, taken off one of the sixteenth-century doors of the original farm-house. There are also copies of portraits of Scott and Dora Wordsworth and an original picture painted by Sir George Beaumont and given by him to William. From the windows can be seen the long ridge which climbs via Low and High Pike to the summit of Fairfield.

At the foot of the stairs is a portrait of the famous headmaster of Rugby, Dr Thomas Arnold, who became a close friend and neighbour, and some engravings by David Law of local views. An arresting photocopy of a sentence in Wordsworth's own hand reads, 'I often ask myself what will become of Rydal Mount after our day.' It must be very pleasing for his great-great-granddaughter to re-read this, sure in the knowledge that he would have approved greatly of the house once again being in the hands of his family. There is also a portrait of one of the earlier owners of the house, John Keene, in whose day the property was known simply as 'Keene's'. It was later known as 'High House' before being given its present name by the Ford Norths.

The drawing-room and library now form one large, handsome L-shaped room with two large windows looking out onto the terrace. It is easy to see where the dividing wall was, and a print hanging in the drawing-room portion makes it doubly clear. From this picture there is evidence that the far wall of the drawing-room was lined with books from floor to ceiling, and a glimpse through the open door leading into the library proper shows rows and rows of books.

Above the fireplace at the library end of the room is a portrait of Dorothy done in 1833 by S. Crosthwaite. Dora refers to this in a letter of the time: Dorothy 'has been sitting for her portrait to a Mr Crossthwaite, a self-educated artist from Cockermouth. (We did not expect much but he has done wonders and delighted us all with an excellent likeness and such a pretty picture). She is taken just as she is now, sitting in the large chair with paper-case on her knee and pen and ink on the table on the one side and "Little Miss Belle" on the other looking so pert and funny.' 'Little Miss Belle' was their dog.

The striking painting of Dora is by Miss Rainbeck, and shows her in bridesmaid's dress. Dora was a devoted companion to her father as she grew up and, despite suffering from a latent form of tuberculosis from the age of eighteen, strove to lead a normal life. She married a friend of the family, Edward Quillinan, in 1841, somewhat against Wordsworth's wishes. Her death in 1847 left him quite distraught.

On the top of a chest of drawers is a Margaret Gillies watercolour on ivory showing William and Mary seated at a table. A similar painting is in Dove Cottage, but this one is set in a free-standing three-sided frame.

The two large portraits of the Monkhouse children (relatives of Mary) have their modern counterparts on the mantelpiece, where there are several photographs of the present owner's grandchildren. Between the two windows is a copy of the Northcote portrait of Coleridge.

The portrait over the other fireplace is by Inman and shows Wordsworth at the age of seventy-four. Henry Inman was an American artist commissioned to paint a portrait which is now in the library of the University of Pennsylvania. Mary was so delighted with the result that she asked him to paint another, which is the one here. While staying at Rydal Mount, the American artist painted a fine study of the outside of the house, a photograph of which hangs close by.

Much of the furniture, including the tables and chairs, was owned by the Wordsworths. On one table is a charming statuette owned by William, which he called 'The Curious Child', showing an infant sitting on the ground with fishes lying at his feet and a fishing-net entangled around one of his legs, a remarkably naturalistic study. The appropriateness of this is made clear by a passage in Book IV of 'The Excursion':

> . . . I have seen
> A curious child, who dwelt upon a tract
> Of inland ground, applying to his ear
> The convolutions of a smooth-lipped shell;
> To which, in silence hushed, his very soul
> Listened intensely; and his countenance soon
> Brightened with joy; for from within were heard
> Murmurings, whereby the monitor expressed
> Mysterious union with its native sea.

The other three-dimensional work in this room is the bust of Wordsworth in the far corner, by his large sofa. Close by are more paintings, including some further fine studies on ivory by Margaret Gillies, the first woman to become a member of the Watercolour Society. There is also a rather sad and gaunt-looking portrait by Thomas Heathfield Carrick of Wordsworth at the age of seventy-seven. This watercolour on marble was executed while 'Mr Wordsworth was under great depression of spirits from the recent loss of his daughter.' The several engravings taken from pictures by John Constable were actually owned by Wordsworth: poet and painter became good friends and much admired each others' works. Of particular interest is the sketch made of the poet's grave in Grasmere Churchyard, painted on 12 August 1850, less than four months after his death. (To regular visitors to Grasmere Churchyard it is a scene which is curiously disconcerting: the accuracy of the study is recognizable, but at the same time there seems to be something missing, for one has become accustomed to seeing the gravestone surrounded by other stones of different members of the family who died several years later.) There is a portrait by Claude Harrison of the great-grandson of William, Christopher William Wordsworth, who died in 1965.

The large glass cabinet contains many personal items which bring to life the day-to-day activities of the Rydal Mount ménage: the picnic box, the grand letter-case marked on the lock 'W Wordsworth Esquire Rydal', a breakfast condiment set, all at variance with the image of 'plain living and high thinking', a prayer book, inkstand, rushlight holder, cigar box and some silver service. A splendid top hat in tip-top condition and a marvellous old leather dispatch-box and small trunk all effuse an air of Victorian gentility and confidence.

A visit on any day of the week and at any time of year to these two rooms is always impressive, but some visitors are privileged to experience these rooms in an unforgettable light – the light of candles and generously loaded log fires. These candlelight evenings were the inspired idea of the custodians, Don and Christine Brookes, and they provide a moving and powerful setting for visitors who wish to have an added dimension to their travels in the steps of the poet. Although the family is associated with the landscape outside, they must have spent many many hours at Rydal under these recreated conditions of flickering lights casting long shadows in all directions, and somehow a glimpse of the candle-lit rooms offers an extra insight into what their daily life must have been like in the long Lakeland winters.

The framed topographical prints on the stairs are of particular interest for those embarking on a tour of the Wordsworth Country. The horizontal lake panoramas by W. Westall, autographed 'To W Wordsworth Esquire', are redolent with the names of houses and beauty spots associated with the poet's friends: Calgarth, Brathay, Greta Hall, Dale End, Allan Bank ('Many years the residence of Mr Wordsworth', reads the printed legend), Applethwaite and Elleray. Westall worked on the originals of these prints whilst staying at Rydal Mount, and Wordsworth has written on one of them, 'This set of prints was given to him by the artist and hung in the drawing room. They are in the original frames.'

The engraving of the Keswick area and Derwentwater, or Keswick Lake as it is here referred to, show how comparatively few buildings were there during that time. Similarly the study of the Vale of Grasmere shows a church still covered in the whitewash which Dorothy had so hoped the heavy rains would wash away, and the island has fewer trees but many more sheep, descendants presumably of the very ones which Dorothy always so regretted disturbing on their picnic jaunts to the island. Appropriately enough, the engraving of Ullswater is from Gowbarrow, where Dorothy and William had come so suddenly and joyously on the hosts of golden daffodils. In the foreground are some superbly antlered stags. These images really do capture the spirit of the countryside at a moment when mass tourism was a generation away.

The first bedroom to be entered is labelled 'William's and Mary's Bedroom', and it comes as something of a surprise to find two single beds made up and ready for use.

For one of the particularly satisfying features of these rooms is that they are still used by descendants of the family, both for themselves and for their guests. The house has very much that indefinable but welcome sense of being 'lived in'. From the window there are fine views of Windermere Lake as far as Bowness Bay, even more distinct in the evening when the lights of that lakeside resort twinkle in the night air. Above the fireplace are portraits of Queen Victoria and the Prince of Wales (later Edward VII) presented by the Queen to Wordsworth while he was Poet Laureate.

There is also a copy of a portrait of the Scottish poet James Hogg, known as 'the Ettrick Shepherd'. The death of Hogg in 1835 triggered a late flowering of Wordsworth's genius, long after many of his most famous works had been completed, in a moving poem which deserves a place of honour among the greatest elegies in our language. Its title must rank among the most unlikely to be appended to a great poem – 'Extempore Effusion on the Death of James Hogg', but it does accurately convey the mode of composition. It was written almost instantly Wordsworth heard of Hogg's death, and the final published version is virtually unchanged from the original composition. He apparently read of his fellow poet's death in the *Newcastle Journal* which had been brought by a visitor to Rydal Mount, and that newspaper was the first to publish the elegy. In fact Wordsworth was no great friend or admirer of Hogg, but the news of the latter's death brought forcibly to his mind the many close friends who had died in recent years, notably Coleridge and Scott. There are also references in the poem to Charles Lamb, 'The frolic and the gentle', Felicia Hemans and George Crabbe. Wordsworth, now sixty-five, had to contemplate the deaths not only of several contemporaries but also of several friends and acquaintances younger than himself:

> Yet I, whose lids from infant slumber
> Were earlier raised, remain to hear
> A timid voice, that asks in whispers,
> 'Who next will drop and disappear?'

Thus does the poem transcend the death of Hogg to become a lament for many deaths and for death in general. This is perhaps an appropriate moment to recall Mary's life at Rydal Mount, for she outlived both William and Dorothy and continued to live on at the house until her own death in 1859, nine years after William's death and four years after Dorothy's. William pays her a fine tribute:

> A perfect woman nobly planned
> To warn, to comfort, to command
> And yet a spirit too, and bright
> With something of an angel light.

He acknowledged that Mary had provided what he considered to be the best two lines in his poem on the daffodils:

> They flash upon that inward eye
> Which is the bliss of solitude.

There is ample evidence that others found her an admirable woman. De Quincey wrote of her 'radiant gracefulness', and Crabb Robinson considered her 'faultless'.

Leaving this room, there are two small steps into an alcove which offers entry to either Dora's room or the room known as Dorothy's room. Dora's is the smallest room open to the public on this floor, and the tiny window is exactly above the front porch. On a desk in the room is an extract from a letter written by Dorothy dated 1818 which refers to Dora's lack of progress in Latin, although she was a good French scholar and 'much improved in many important points'. This letter tells of the plans for converting the outhouse, which in the summer now serves as the ticket office and bookshop for visitors to the Mount: 'We are going to make a schoolroom, and a very nice one it will be. The saddle room above the stable. I'm sure you will rejoice at the contrivance.'

Dorothy's room next door is also still used as a bedroom for guests. The walls are decorated with prints and paintings of landscapes, and there are two windows enjoying different aspects. One looks over the front garden, and the other is placed on the side wall of the house and looks out to the ridge which is part of the fell-walk known as the Fairfield Horseshoe.

Up a further flight of stairs is Wordsworth's attic study, which contains an engaging and eclectic mixture of memorabilia. By one window is the sword which belonged to his brother John, drowned when his East Indiaman *Earl of Abergavenny* was shipwrecked. The sword was presented to him for the part he played in a campaign against the French. A copy of the citation records that the sword cost £50.

An exceptionally thorough family tree practically covers one wall and shows various branches of the Wordsworths. These include two Wordsworths who became Bishops of Lincoln and St Andrews. These two descendants, Charles and Christopher, were at Oxford and Cambridge respectively and a small panel notes that they both rowed, and that in 1829 Charles rowed in the first Oxford and Cambridge Boat Race and is credited with the founding of this famous event.

Another curiosity is a Press cutting which goes back to 1872 when a correspondent to the *Daily Telegraph* expressed great concern that on a visit to Rydal Mount he found the gate padlocked and a large private sign repelling prospective visitors. The letter-writer explains that he had entered the grounds by an open side gate before seeing the sign. 'The house is at present tenantless and undergoing repair and no one happened to be present to hinder me from me going through my devotions at the shrine of my favourite poet. As I wandered through the grounds however I was stopped by the growl of a dog. The owner had chained the cur in a spot where he could bite such pilgrims as myself. I ask the public sir whether this is quite right? Because I go to see the place where Wordsworth lived and died am I to be bitten by an unaesthetic mongrel?'

Among this pot-pourri of memorabilia is a more lengthy cutting, and this time from a learned journal published for a very specialized readership. This is an extract from *The Optician* magazine dated 1 March 1968. Why it should be here is apparent from the title of the essay on display; 'Some Observations on the Sight of William Wordsworth', which makes a scientific diagnosis of the eye complaint which dogged the poet for so many years and which was capable of reducing him to misery, rendering all reading and writing impossible. The blue stone now on view at Dove Cottage which gave him considerable relief when applied to his eyelids is referred to in the article, as well as a comment on the efficacy of 'some very superior eyeshades' which he acquired to give him further relief.

Dorothy in her spells of invalidity paints some vivid word-pictures of the daily round at Rydal: the doves out basking in the sunshine as their gardener tends the gooseberry bushes; the end of a long winter heralded one morning by the cry of the hounds and the welcome sight of the early primroses. The compensation for a harsh and bitter winter was the joys of ice skating, for in her brother's sixtieth year Dorothy asserts that he is still 'the crack skater' she must have often admired in their youth; there are references to cosy fireside chats and to copious winter reading. But despite these delights, it was the summer which always gave the family their greatest joys. This was the time of the year when they would encourage visitors to stay with them, or at least to lodge in nearby houses.

Wordsworth wrote that in summer they were often 'full to overflowing'; hence the necessity of finding rented accommodation for some of their friends in Rydal. The summer of 1831 for instance passed in a 'fever of pleasure' with regattas on Windermere, grand balls, picnics and long walks.

Today the marvellous gardens at Rydal Mount receive at least as much praise as the house, and sometimes more. Over many years Wordsworth devoted a great deal of time, thought and energy to planning the grounds, and the family's letters are full of proud and excited references to the building of the successive terraces. They were all keenly interested in their garden, and indeed in the gardens of their neighbours and friends far and near. Wordsworth had decided views on the laying out of grounds, and he acknowledged that the longest letter he ever wrote in his life was to Sir George Beaumont, giving him detailed advice on the landscaping of his winter garden in Leicestershire.

So Wordsworth would have greatly approved of the care which is now bestowed on the 4½ acres at Rydal Mount. He was a firm believer in the informal garden which harmonized with the surrounding countryside, with '. . . lawn, and trees carefully planted so as not to obscure the view'. There was a vegetable garden in his time, and he either improved or constructed three terraces, a source of much enjoyment. The sloping terrace is thought to have been a feature of the grounds long before the Wordsworths moved in to the Mount, but the summer house at the end of this walk was built by William. Here he would often retreat to enjoy 'the innocent sweetness of a new born day'.

Just as Dorothy had looked 'with pride and partiality' on their garden at Grasmere, so too did she take a great deal of interest in the developing grounds at Rydal, so much more extensive than those of their previous homes. Her letters go into considerable detail about the improvements being carried out; the work on their grounds kindled an almost obsessive enthusiasm in their breasts. She took special pleasure in the late colours which they often enjoyed, well into September with '. . . potentilla climbing up every green bush, Asters, Dalias etc etc – and not forgetting the humble pansy – purple and yellow'.

At this period, the late 1820s and early 30s, Dorothy was dogged by bad health and not infrequently housebound. She was taken round the garden and the lower, recently constructed terrace in a bath chair which had belonged to Mrs Curwen of Belle Isle. How ironic this fact appears in contrast with her youthful and animated visit to Belle Isle, the Windermere island, in her Dove Cottage days. How impatient she must have felt as they carried her up and down those steps. She referred to these outings as her 'baby rides' and came to accept them as a wonderful alternative to being confined to the house and the immediate vicinity of the building.

The Wordsworths' zest for the outdoor life, even in the

face of troublesome illnesses, was always impressive.
William's eye complaint could be so acute that he was
unable to savour the simplest of pleasures: '. . . my eyes
would not allow me to gaze upon dazzling water . . .' he
wrote to Pickersgill, the portrait-painter who came to stay
at Rydal and whom he urged to 'travel on the outside of the
coach for the sake of the very fine views'. He would sit out
in the summer house at all times of the day when the
weather would allow, and he certainly did not confine
himself only to the balmy days of high summer, as one
poem illustrates, a poem which was composed one evening
'when the wind was blowing high':

> What pensive beauty autumn shows,
> Before she hears the sound
> Of winter rushing in, to close
> The emblematic round!
>
> Such be our Spring, our Summer such;
> So may our Autumn blend
> With hoary Winter, and life touch,
> Through heaven-born hope, her end!

4

The Darling Vales

Hawkshead, Esthwaite, Windermere
Ambleside and Langdale

To say that Wordsworth left a lasting impression on his
school at Hawkshead is to state a literal truth: along with
generations of other schoolboys he carved his name on his
desk, a signature which can still be seen today and one
which has the singular distinction of being protected from
further carvings by a small glass frame cunningly set into
the surrounding wood. This was in the days long before the
fountain and ball-point pen, when boys were obliged to
carry knives to sharpen their quills if they were to avoid
'blotting their copybook'. Few seem to have resisted the
temptation to use their blades in a fashion for which,
though not designed for this purpose, they were clearly
effective. Every inch of every desk-top is now covered with
signatures.

Wordsworth remained deeply grateful for his schooling
at Hawkshead, which in his time (he arrived at Whitsun
in 1779, aged nine) enjoyed a splendid reputation for
scholarship. The school was founded by Archbishop
Sandys in 1585, a fact of more than incidental importance
in that his earliest known verse was an exercise set by the
masters to celebrate the bicentenary of the school's foundation. By Wordsworth's own admission, this task '. . .
put it into my head to compose verses from the impulse
of my own mind'. He acknowledged that this early
attempt at poetry, although much admired, was a 'tame
imitation of Pope's versification', but even so, for a boy

of fourteen it already shows an admirable command of words:

> And has the Sun his flaming chariot driven
> Two hundred times around the ring of heaven,
> Since Science first, with all her sacred train,
> Beneath yon roof began her heavenly reign?

This lofty style continues for another hundred or so lines, and the reader can be in no doubt that the writer was almost intoxicated by the excitement of his composition, revelling in his inventive use of rhyme, personification and phrasing.

To step inside the school today is to be immediately transported back to Wordsworth's time, for the building is thoughtfully cared for by an enthusiastic and knowledgable custodian who sees the school not only as a shrine for Wordsworthians but also a monument to generations of children who have spent their formative years under this 'happy roof'.

Immediately on the right inside the main door is the desk which boasts the signature of the future Poet Laureate, who incidentally never lost his zest for carving words on trees, writing on stones and slate and composing epitaphs. A sense of history hits one at once. The long, uncomfortable wooden benches of the scholars and the original teacher's desk seem at first austere, but this impression is softened by the large open fireplace, the poignant list of past masters, and the texts around the walls, most appropriately the phrase which Wordsworth was to make famous long before Freud came into the consciousness of present-day pilgrims: 'The Child is Father of the Man.'

A stone staircase leads to an upper room, perhaps the headmaster's tiny study, and a few steps higher is another classroom which now contains a fascinating collection of documents and exhibits relating to the building's distinguished history. Adjoining this room is what must have been the school's pride and joy – the library, with its remarkable collection of books. Indeed, over forty years after Wordsworth had left the school, his sister Dorothy used the excellence of Hawkshead's library as a means of inducing their nephew Christopher to spend part of his vacation from university with them in the Lake District.

It was a tradition for the boys on leaving to make a gift of a book to the library, and many continued this generous practice throughout their lives. The original collection was started by Daniel Rawlinson in 1675. He was a local boy who became a successful London vintner and who supplied wine to Samuel Pepys. He seems to have been equally successful in persuading his friends to donate books to the library, which was augmented substantially in 1789. Thus Wordsworth had ample opportunity to read widely, and when he went up to St John's, Cambridge, he found himself well ahead of his contemporaries in many subjects.

The exterior is worth a close look. The picturesque sandstone architraves and mullioned windows were added in 1891 by Lieutenant-Colonel Myles Sandys of Graythwaite Hall, a descendant of the Archbishop who founded the school and whose family still occupy Graythwaite Hall. Above the school door a plaque records the work of Rawlinson, and above that a sundial shows the progress of young William's 'flaming chariot'. The gardens at Graythwaite are open to the public in spring and early summer, when their stunningly impressive azaleas and rhododendrons are in their full glory.

Behind and above the school, the church, in Wordsworth's words, sits

> . . . like a throned lady sending out
> A gracious look all over her domain.

As one would expect from a school founded by an Archbishop of York, religious instruction was part of the curriculum, along with Latin, Greek and mathematics. Considering the long day the children had to endure, it seems amazing that William ever found time for all the early morning walks he records in 'The Prelude'. In the summer months they were at their desks by 6.30 a.m., and they remained at school until at least 6 p.m. with a two-hour break at midday. Attendance at church was strictly enforced on Sundays and holy days.

The church is also a fine historical building. Dedicated to St Michael and All Angels, it commands a most spectacular view of the surrounding countryside. To the north is the Fairfield Range, and stretching out beyond the crowded village rooftops is the flat vale through which Black Beck flows into Esthwaitewater, then the distinctive outline of Latterbarrow, a hill which all Hawkshead school children must find irresistible with its sugar-loaf shape and the tall, circular cairn which graces its summit. Wordsworth often visited the churchyard on summer evenings to look at the grave of an eleven-year-old schoolboy whose untimely death made a great impression on him:

> A long half-hour together I have stood
> Mute – looking at the grave in which he lies.

He must also have frequently admired the panorama which can still be enjoyed from this easy vantage-point: Coniston Old Man, Helvellyn, Kirkstone, Ill Bell and the heavily wooded Claife Heights with its string of evocatively named tarns – Wise Een, Moss Eccles, Three Dubs and Wray Mires. When the Duke of Edinburgh paid an official visit to the Lake District in 1966, one of his duties was to perform the official opening of a waymarked walk along the Heights, which had long been a notorious place for ramblers losing their way. Wordsworth would surely have approved, for one of his greatest pleasures was to walk in the countryside of this area 'pre-eminent in beauty'.

Many visitors around Wordsworth's time at Hawkshead were struck by the brilliant whitewash which covered the church's outside walls; he himself referred to the 'snow white church', and another late eighteenth-century observer writes of the 'milk-white tower'. Today of course this rough-cast is gone (it was removed during the restoration of 1875), and the stonework can be seen, presumably quarried locally as it consists of the Silurian stone which gives such a distinctive 'pastoral' character to the countryside surrounding Esthwaitewater and Windermere. This stone is not, however, the best medium for a mason intent on decorative and ornate detail, and so, as in the Grammar School, the doors and windows make use of the red sandstone found all round the fringes of the Lake District.

Inside the building is further evidence of the local geology. The blue flags in the nave and south porch were certainly there at the time Wordsworth and his brothers attended for worship. So too were the murals, although some have been revealed only in more recent times. Biblical texts reminiscent of the church at Grasmere are surrounded by round and oval abstract borders, and coloured dog-tooth patterns adorn several of the bulky columns and arches; underneath one arch the names of four men are remembered:

> Church Wardens for Ye year 1711
> Anthony Hall of Wray
> Job Sawrey of Hollinbank
> Wm. Satterth'wt
> Adam Taylor of Hawkshead.

One of the most interesting church records in the region hangs in a frame by the north door. It is a 'Burial in Woolen' Certificate and recalls the paramount importance in times past of the wool trade, not only for the Lake District but also for much of England. It is also a touching reminder of the widespread illiteracy in the seventeenth century, as the witnesses, unable to write or even spell their names, have been obliged to sign with a cross mark. The certificate testifies to the fact that the corpse of Margaret Tyson '. . . was not put in wrapt or wound up or buried in any shirt sheet shrift or shroud made or mingled with flax hemp etc or any coffin lined with cloth or any other material but what is made of sheep wool onlie according to a late Act of Parliament made for burying in woolen'. The Parliamentary Act referred to was passed in 1666 in order to foster the wool trade. The framed example is sealed and dated 1696, and the Agnes and Dorothy Tyson who witnessed the affidavit with 'this their mark X' may well have been ancestors of Ann Tyson's husband who provided board for the Wordsworth children.

As William and the other hundred or so boys who attended the school at this time sat through the prayers and sermons, their attention must frequently have wandered, perhaps first to the murals of 'sentences from Scripture decently Flourished' or to the Sandys Chapel containing the table tombs and life-size effigies of members of this eminent local family. More likely still the boys thought about their wild adventures in the surrounding countryside. William admitted that 'we were a noisy crew', even though he himself had a taste for the quieter pursuits. In the spring, perhaps he found his way to the aptly named Cuckoo Brow Wood on Claife Heights to track down that often heard but seldom seen bird:

> The same whom in my schoolboy days
> I listened to; that Cry
> Which made me look a thousand ways
> In bush, and tree, and sky.
>
> To seek thee did I often rove
> Through woods and on the green;
> And thou wert still a hope, a love;
> Still longed for, never seen.

The boys were expected to work hard in school, and they seem to have been equally energetic in their play, if Wordsworth's poems are a reliable guide. For instance he would walk or ride considerable distances, visiting, among other places, Grasmere, Ings and Furness Abbey. Nutting was a favourite pursuit in the autumn, and they enjoyed rowing, bird-nesting and ice-skating, a pastime Wordsworth continued well into his old age, often skating at night by the light of the moon and the stars:

> All shod with steel,
> We hissed along the polished ice in games
> Confederate, imitative of the chase. . . .

Just as they were allowed considerable freedom for play, so too were they encouraged to read widely. William read most of Fielding's novels and Swift's *Gulliver's Travels* and recalled many years later how he had read 'with great pleasure' Gilbert White's *Natural History of Selborne*.

For over a century experts have tried to identify the cottage in Hawkshead where William and his three brothers lodged. For many years the accolade went to a charming house tucked away off the village square. All the brochures, postcards and tea-towels show this as the Wordsworth lodgings, and a somewhat battered metal road sign at the edge of the village still boasts of this connection. However, when Mrs Heelis (alias Beatrix Potter of *Peter Rabbit* fame) discovered the Tyson account books, scholarly opinion adduced that the boys had in fact lived at the nearby hamlet of Colthouse. For many years, to come down in favour of one or the other was to incur the wrath of the rival factions – something which those familiar with the enmities which lurk within the groves of academe are understandably loath to do. It is now agreed that Wordsworth lived in *both* Hawkshead and Colthouse, as it seems that Ann Tyson moved from Hawkshead to Colthouse during the very period that he lodged with her. What has never been in doubt is the kindliness of the 'aged dame' who became a second mother to the Wordsworth boys.

A delightful picture of life at the Tysons' emerges from the references in Book I of 'The Prelude'. There were the 'home amusements' by a bright peat fire, playing noughts and crosses on a slate and engaging in such games as whist and loo with the ferocity and intensity which today's youngsters reserve for the electronic video games:

> Oh! with what echoes on the board they fell.
> Ironic Diamonds, Clubs, Hearts . . .
> . . . precipitated down
> With Scoffs and taunts . . . .

These were happy days, and when Wordsworth left Hawkshead for the University of Cambridge, he must have had mixed feelings. Certainly on his return during the summer vacation he is glad to acknowledge the debt he owes to 'my old Dame, so motherly and good ... with a parent's pride'.

With the recent pedestrianization of the centre of Hawkshead, it is easy enough to re-create mentally the scene which awaited Wordsworth on his return. Many bewail the commercialization of the village, but much of interest remains. The quaint architecture and curious alleys surely make this the most picturesque village in Lakeland. Like most travellers who return to their childhood haunts after a period of absence, Wordsworth re-marked how much smaller everything seemed: 'So narrow seemed the brooks, the fields so small.' But if the fields seemed small, they still held powerful memories for one who had in his own words been 'fostered alike by beauty and by fear'.

On the road which leads away from the church, past the gates of the school (ignoring the left-hand curve of the road which leads towards the large car-park), after a few hundred yards, there is a road junction by some cottages and an old water-pump. On the left is a footpath across the fields which Wordsworth so enjoyed and which arrives in a short while at the shores of Esthwaitewater. No matter how crowded are the streets left behind, here there is guaranteed peace, quiet and beauty. The path along the lakeshore to the right leads to the Nab, a promontory from which there is a splendid view and from which the lake looks much vaster than it truly is. The rocks by the shore are the kind of spot which the young Wordsworth sought out in order to experience that peace 'which passeth all understanding'. At sunrise one may share more readily his overwhelming sense of calm:

> Nor seldom did I lift the cottage latch
> And ere one Smoke-wreath had risen
> From dwelling, or the thrush
> Piped to the woods his shrill reveille, sate
> Alone upon some jutting eminence,
> At the first gleam of dawn light, when the vale
> Yet slumbering, lay in utter solitude.

Oft in these moments such a holy calm
Would overspread my soul, that bodily eyes
Were utterly forgotten, and what I saw
Appeared like something in myself, a dream
A prospect in the mind.

The outlying hamlet of Colthouse is half a mile to the east of the main village, a picturesque cluster of houses. The Wordsworth children lodged at Green End Cottage, which fits more accurately most of the poetic references to Ann Tyson's home. From the open door on a summer evening William would gaze out onto a 'copse-clad bank' and indulge his rich imagination, seeing shapes and pictures in the way, more usually, one might see patterns in clouds:

'Twas now for me a burnished silver shield
Suspended over a knight's tomb, who lay
Inglorious, buried in the dusky wood. . . .

Eileen Jay, a Wordsworth scholar living in Colthouse, has convincingly identified this as Spring Wood, and other references leave no doubt that Colthouse was the home of much of William's childhood.

Explorations on and around Windermere, England's longest lake, could not begin at a more appropriate place than Belle Isle, the largest of Windermere's islands and the only one to be inhabited. It came eventually to be one of the favourite retreats of the Wordsworths. But not when Wordsworth was writing his *Guide to The Lakes*. Here he reserved his only reference in the *Guide* to Belle Isle for the chapter sub-headed 'Causes of False Taste in Grounds and Buildings'. Today most visitors would agree that it is quite one of the most romantic places in the Lake District, and after William's son John married into the family who owned it (the Curwens), the Wordsworths' criticism abated as they came to know the island home better. William objected to the embanking of the shores, which he thought destroyed the natural appearance of the island:

'Could not the margin of this noble island be given back to Nature? Winds and waves work with a careless and graceful hand: and should they in some places carry away a portion of the soil, the trifling loss would be amply compensated by the additional spirit, dignity, and loveliness, which these agents and other powers of Nature would soon communicate to what was left behind.' When it was first built, the house was dismissed as a 'pepperpot', though it is now valued not only for being the first round house to be built in England but also for its beautiful and ingenious design.

When the Reverend John Wordsworth became betrothed to the heiress of Belle Isle, Isabella Curwen, there was much intercourse between Belle Isle and Rydal Mount. Dora thought the spot delightful, but Dorothy was never absolutely convinced that living on a thirty-acre island was advisable. She thought that the inhabitants 'persuaded themselves' that there really was no more trouble to living on an island and having to be ferried to the shore than in walking the same distance. She grudgingly conceded that it was a 'splendid place', and in 1832 it was also a place of refuge, Isabella spending the summer there to avoid the cholera which had swept through her main home at Workington.

The middle part of Windermere has associations with Wordsworth stretching right back to his Hawkshead schooldays, and he remembered vividly going on 'nutting' forays in the woods on the west shore. Dressed in the most ragged clothes which his 'frugal dame' kept specifically for such activities, he spent many a long day in this area. In 'The Waggoner' he refers to the owls of the lake:

> Upon the banks of Windermere
> Where a tribe of them makes merry,
> Mocking the man that keeps the ferry.

He frequently used the ferry at this time of his life, and returning to Hawkshead after finishing a term at Cambridge, he could scarce contain his excitement at taking the boat to the west shore:

I bounded down the hill, shouting amain
A lusty summons to the farther shore
For the old Ferryman; and when he came
I did not step into the well known Boat,
Without a cordial welcome. . . .

Today a vehicle ferry still operates regularly across the middle of Windermere, and although it is no longer the most popular route from Kendal to Hawkshead, as it was in Wordsworth's day, it is still a great treat for children unused to such modes of transport.

Although the village of Bowness on Windermere has changed greatly with its development as a major holiday resort and as a destination for coach trips from all over the north of England, there are still pockets of the village where it is possible to recreate the kind of township the Wordsworths knew, which in those days was considerably smaller than the present-day village. Naturally the church has much that is unchanged. Here is the remarkable memorial to Bishop Watson, a close friend of the Wordsworths, which is at the east end of the south aisle. This striking monument consists of a mitre, crozier and books, carved so as to seem that they could almost be taken from the tablet and used in a ceremonial procession. The sculptor of this monument was the famous Flaxman, and the Bishop and his wife are buried outside close by the window near this tablet.

One of the curates of the church was the Reverend John Flemming, with whom Wordsworth had been a pupil at Hawkshead. They remained lifelong friends, and with the passing of the years and the building of several grand houses along this side of the lake, Wordsworth's 'Windermere Circle' increased both in circumference and in grandeur.

Bishop Watson built himself a fine mansion close to the shores of the lake near to the present White Cross Bay Caravan Site. Known as Calgarth Park, it soon became a meeting-place for some of the most influential politicians and men of letters of the day. Prominent among them was Wordsworth, as well as Walter Scott, Christopher North and de Quincey, who described the Bishop as 'a joyous, jovial and cordial host'.

Calgarth Park is now converted into tastefully designed flats for retired professional people, the property having been purchased by the Lake District Branch of the British Federation of University Women. However, it is unlikely that the Bishop would have approved of anything so radical as a university-educated woman. He was noted for his conservative views and was a source of a great deal of patronage. He himself had been at times Professor at Oxford of both Chemistry and Divinity, and it is said that he never visited his see at Llandaff Cathedral, which in any case was roofless and in ruins. The posts to which he appointed his friends and relatives were considered little more than a source of income, and it was said that he was one of the few bishops who could hold a chapter meeting with the majority of his prebends in the comfort of his own library so far away from his cathedral.

Calgarth Park remains the 'elegant mansion' described by West soon after it was built. Dating from 1789, it pleasingly combines level lawns, balustraded terraces and classical columns, with glimpses of the lake. The Bishop planted many of the oak, ash and conifer trees in the area. Wordsworth, out riding this way with Captain Greaves of Ferney Green, describes one of those mornings in the early spring which those who live by Windermere know so well, when a thin grey mist pervades the scene and, although the sun has yet to break through, one may be confident that a fine bright morning is on its way: '. . . soft though sunless, still waters and an indigo tint upon the fells . . . brought into harmony by the grey atmosphere with the lively hues of the budding trees seen to advantage along the tract of Calgarth Woods'. Far less attractive is the image conjured up by Dorothy of an ugly incident which involved the Bishop's washerwoman, who, on returning home from Calgarth with her 9 guineas in wages, was set upon by masked robbers. The fact that the assailants spoke not a word convinced Dorothy that they were locals.

As the interests of tourists in the Lake District increased, so too did the busyness of the Windermere area, which in the early years of the nineteenth century, as it still is today, was quite the most popular part of the Lake District. In 1816, for instance, Wordsworth was writing to his good friend Crabb Robinson, recommending him on his Lakes tour to be sure to seek out a woman who lived on the west shore of the lake near to the Ferry House who would act as a local guide, showing him especially the famed view to be obtained from Mr Curwen's 'pleasure house'. Dorothy was no less conscientious in making plans for visiting friends and relatives. In the summer of 1827 she is busying herself with the arrangements for her three nephews, along with their tutor and other students, to make up a vacation reading-party based at Bowness. She is highly pleased when she secures a three-bedroomed house for 30 shillings a week, including, she stresses, linen and washing and the additional luxury of a sitting-room and fuel for a 'trifle' extra.

Opposite the church at Bowness is a cleverly converted school building now known as Wordsworth Court. When it was re-named and made into holiday flats, some local people derided the name as a gimmick. In fact, there is a close and genuine connection with Wordsworth, for he opened a school nearby and the proprietors discovered the handsome foundation stone which he unveiled and which now graces the front of Wordsworth Court; it is decorated with funerary emblems, a tribute to John Bolton of Storrs Hall, who endowed the school but did not live to see the building completed. The finely wrought inscription tells all:

This medallion and tablet were placed here at the expense of / inhabitants in the township of Applethwaite & Under Millbeck / To testify their gratitude to John Bolton esq / for the great benefit conferred upon the place by his / munificence in providing for the erection of this schoolhouse / and the ornamental disposition of the adjoining ground / It pleased God that the generous benefactor / should depart this life while the building was in progress / and the surrounding funeral emblems are expressive / of natural regret that he did not live to see his work completed/. The foundation was laid April 13th 1836 / by William Wordsworth esq of Rydal

Mount / Mr Bolton died Feb 24th 1837 aged 80 & the school
was opened Sept 20th 1838 / his widow piously fulfilling all
his benevolent designs.

In 'The Prelude' Wordsworth describes a splendid inn
at Bowness which he greatly admired as a boy. It was the
'White Lion', and here on the bowling-green he and his
schoolfriends loved to play, their shouts making 'all the
mountains ring'. Modern Bowness has grown up around
the inn which was renamed the Royal Hotel after the
Dowager Queen Adelaide stayed there in 1840 (she went
on to visit Wordsworth at Rydal Mount). But despite the
changes, traces of the bowling – green can still be seen,
and inside the building one sees how it must have dominated the surrounding area. Even in Wordsworth's time he
had noticed changes, the hotel being 'gentrified' in various
ways, including the replacement of the homely rustic sign
of a lion with a blue-frosted signboard with large golden
characters. He remembers too the strawberries and 'mel-
low cream' with relish, as well as describing a scene of
haunting beauty and atmosphere on the return across the
lake. Apparently it was the family's custom in the dusky
light to land on one of the many small islands which dot
the lake and leave ashore the 'minstrel of the troop' who
would play his flute alone upon the rock, while they rowed
away:

> . . . Oh then the calm
> And dead still water lay upon my mind
> Even with a weight of pleasure, and the sky
> Never before so beautiful, sank down
> Into my heart, and held me like a dream.

All the sojourners on Bowness Promenade gazing at the
summer sunsets are still continuing that tradition.

A little to the south of Bowness is the lakeside mansion
of Storrs Hall, now a spacious hotel and open to non-
residents for lunch and dinner. It is worth the cost of a
meal here simply to enjoy the grounds which the Wordsworths, regular diners at Storrs, knew well. As the home
of Colonel John Bolton, it became a great centre for the

social life of the area, and large dinner parties and grand regattas on the lake were common. One of the Boltons' regular guests was William Huskisson, President of the Board of Trade, whose morose place in history was assured when he became the world's first railway fatality on being knocked down by the engine which drew the first regular passenger service, between Liverpool and Manchester.

In the summer of 1825 Wordsworth attended the regatta at Storrs in honour of their distinguished guests, Walter Scott and George Canning. In the entrance hall to the hotel above a wood fire is a portrait of John Bolton with his King Charles spaniel, dressed in a long bottle-green coat and cravat and with a top hat at his elbow. It affords a glimpse of the colour and variety which must have attended these occasions.

The white house of Storrs has an almost intimidating Doric porch for an entrance on the east side, with a long balcony on the first floor. The decorative motifs are echoed on the other sides of the building, and the grounds enjoy views of lake and hills. Parts of the shore area are graced by fine stands of oak, and at other points rhododendrons make a heady splash of colour in May and June. The much-photographed Storrs Temple should not be missed. This octagonal structure at the end of a substantial jetty is approached through an arched entrance; the three similarly arched windows give views of different aspects of the lake scene. The 'temple' was erected in 1804 in honour of four British admirals: Duncan, St Vincent, Howe and Nelson.

Three miles north of Windermere, towards Ambleside, is the Low Wood Hotel. Originally a coaching inn, it might also have had the benefit of being the terminus of the Kendal–Windermere railway had not Wordsworth and others mounted a concerted campaign against the extension from its present terminus. Nowadays it is a rapidly developing centre for water sports, but to the Wordsworths it was the point where they might collect welcome letters from their friends. It was apparently an inn of some renown, for in 1807 one of the guests was Lady Holland, whom Wordsworth visited in order to gain her support for the fund organized to maintain the orphans of the Green family following the deaths of the children's parents in a blizzard. It was a timely intervention by Wordsworth, for on her return to London Lady Holland was instrumental in persuading many of her acquaintances to make further donations, including gifts from the Dukes of Devonshire and Bedford. Ten years later Dorothy writes to her friend Jane Marshall that she intends to 'stroll down to Winandermere, and shall take a boat for the sake of the sunset over the Langdale mountains, a spectacle I have often heard you speak of with delight'. Wordsworth in his *Guide* and in his letters often strongly recommended the hotel both as a place to stay and for the stunning views of the lake and mountains. It was here in the summer of 1822 that Dorothy attended a regatta at which young John was part of a crew of oarsmen (known as 'the Mountaineers') which took on a crew of undergraduates from Cambridge who were staying in Ambleside.

At the head of the lake on the banks of the River Brathay are two houses with distinguished histories – Old Brathay and Brathay Hall. The Brathay Estate is now the base for Expeditionary Activities and for an environmental field-study centre. Old Brathay was the home of Charles Lloyd and his family, great favourites with the Wordsworths. Dorothy used to spend time here from Rydal Mount in order to take care of the Lloyds' eight children, and Dora at one time visited them three times a week for dancing lessons, often staying to enjoy the fun and companionship of her contemporaries. One of the children – Owen, born in 1803, became the curate of the church of Langdale at Chapel Stile. Charles Lloyd's sister Priscilla married William's younger brother Christopher, so there was the additional bond of family connection to bind the two households together. It must have also been comforting to know that friendly folk were now ensconced in Old Brathay, since it had once been occupied by two 'flashy brothers' who were hanged for highway robbery. Sir George Beaumont, Wordsworth's early patron, had also taken the house for a time.

At the neighbouring Brathay Hall lived John Harden,

an Irishman with a gift for painting. Many of his canvases offer a unique glimpse into the everyday lives of the local population during the Wordsworths' time. It was here that Wordsworth probably met John Constable, the great landscape painter. Again the younger members of both families were great friends. When the Hardens moved to Field Head House, nearer to Hawkshead, Dr Arnold and his family rented the house for the summer of 1832.

From the road by Brathay Bridge there are tantalizing glimpses of the estate, but on the banks of the Brathay by the Roman Fort at Waterhead, there are views across the fine wooded grounds.

As the Wordsworth children grew up, and especially after their father was appointed Distributor of Stamps (in effect a local tax-collector), Ambleside seems to have become more important in their lives. Here was their nearest doctor, and here was Miss Dowling's school, attended for three years by Dorothy before she went to school in Appleby. Hartley and Derwent Coleridge attended Mr Dawes' school, and some years later Hartley was to become one of the undistinguished teachers, noted for his lack of discipline and disorganized methods. Wordsworth's Stamp Office was on the corner of Church Street, close to the present bakery shop. It is still known as the Old Stamp House.

Today's fell-walkers, looking down on the town from Loughrigg or Wansfell, must often remark on how frequently mist or smoke lingers over Ambleside's buildings on otherwise clear mornings, a point which Wordsworth made the theme for a sonnet:

> Deep in the vale a little rural Town
> Breathes forth a cloud-like creature of its own,
> That mounts not toward the radiant morning sky,
> But, with a less ambitious sympathy,
> Hangs o'er its Parent waking to the cares,
> Troubles and toils that every day prepares. . . .

It is clear too that, since the Wordsworths' day, Ambleside has considerably expanded, largely to accommodate the growing tourist industry. The town was formerly divided into two parishes by Stock Beck – Grasmere and Windermere. The church on the hill in the old part of the town was in use within living memory but is now the village hall. This church of St Anne dates largely from 1812 and was on the site of a much older chapel, which was described as 'decayed and damp and almost past using'. It was thought that no artist's impression of this older chapel existed until a scholar compared a sketch by Wordsworth's patron, Sir George Beaumont, of a church with crow-stepped gables with another, older engraving simply entitled 'Church near Ambleside'. Although the two studies at first looked very different, the scholar realized that the engraving must have been inadvertently reversed so that, when Beaumont's 1806 study is compared with a mirror reflection of the earlier engraving, they are clearly the same building.

Attractive though the church appears, with its stepped bell turret and irregularly spaced windows, it was apparently inconvenient to worship in, to say the least, and there are tales of the roof being so leaky that an umbrella was a necessary accessory for those wishing to attend divine service in anything approaching comfort. Perhaps one day the long-lost bell will be discovered. It was rung so vigorously to announce the victory of Nelson at the Battle of the Nile that it cracked.

In many ways the old church presents a sad spectacle.* A notice over a door close to the tower reads somewhat incongruously, 'Licensed in pursuant of Act of Parliament for public music, dancing or other public entertainment of the like kind'. The churchyard is woefully neglected, and among the seemingly forgotten graves is a shaped headstone, overgrown with brambles. It is largely illegible, but the name John Dawes is discernible. This is the Reverend Dawes whose school was attended by two of Coleridge's children for a time. The school eventually failed, and Dawes' erratic behaviour gave the Wordsworths cause for concern. Wordsworth refers to Dawes' extreme irritability of nerve and his many contradictions and changes of

* In 1984 the church was converted into residential flats.

purpose. But he still deserves that his grave be better cared for. Set into the stone is a long brass plaque with the names of some twenty subscribers to this memorial. It reads like a roll-call of the Wordsworth circle of the time and includes Ford North, John Harden, John Wordsworth, Derwent Coleridge, John Flemming, Owen Lloyd, John Crump and of course William Wordsworth himself.

The newer church of St Mary the Virgin, with its dominating spire, was designed by Gilbert Scott and completed in 1854. Mary Wordsworth, by then a widow of four years, was present at the consecration, and presented a lectern and a Bible, inscribed in her own hand, which was in use until 1968, when it was placed in a glass cabinet. Although Wordsworth had died before work on the new church had begun, he took a great interest in the plans and gave generously to the cost of the building. Admirers of his work at home and in America subscribed to the cost of the memorial window at the east end of the north aisle. From the earliest days of the church, this has always been referred to as the Wordsworth Chapel. Here too are windows to the memory of Mary, Dora and Dorothy, each bearing the family motto, '*Veritas*'.

The charming mural is of the Ambleside Rushbearing, which shares a similar history with that of Grasmere and takes a similar form. It is held each year on a Saturday in July, and its traditional hymn was composed by Owen Lloyd, a life-long friend of the Wordsworths. The east window, with its five lights showing the four evangelists and St Paul, was the gift of a distant Wordsworth relative, Mrs Benson Harrison. Before her marriage she was known as 'middle' Dorothy Wordsworth to avoid confusion; she was the youngest daughter of William's first cousin, Richard, married the ironmaster Benson Harrison and lived at Green Bank, now part of Charlotte Mason College.

There is a pleasant walk through the park close to St Mary's Church across a bridge over the River Rothay and onto the Under Loughrigg road, much more important a century ago than it is today. This road hugs the right bank of the Rothay as it tumbles towards Windermere, carrying the clear waters of Rydalwater and Grasmere into the Brathay. Along the road are a number of interesting houses. Turning right, towards Pelter Bridge at Rydal, on the right is Fox How, which can be glimpsed through its grand iron gates. Here Dr Thomas Arnold of Rugby School built his home, helped and, one often fears, hindered by Wordsworth's advice and suggestions. The distinctive round chimneys on the house, and those of others in the area, are due largely to Wordsworth's influence. It was designed as a vacation-time retreat for the Arnold family, and once the house was completed, Dr Arnold and Wordsworth spent a good deal of time together planning out the garden and deciding on the trees and shrubs to be planted. Even after the doctor's death, the family continued to keep up the house, and a friendship developed between Wordsworth and Matthew Arnold, a great admirer of his poetry.

Fox Ghyll, a short distance away, also has connections with the Rydal Mount household. This was the home successively of Robert Blakeney, de Quincey and Mrs Luff, the Wordsworths' friend of earlier years. Even before Blakeney had moved in, Wordsworth was interfering with comments about the design of the house and grounds which again amount almost to an obsession. He was clearly taken with what seems to have been an innovation in house design, incorporating french windows, the detailed description of which he sent to Blakeney. This suggests they were not nearly so common in their time as now. Perhaps the unusual glass porch which is so prominent a feature of Fox Ghyll today dates back to this influence. But if Blakeney found Wordsworth a tiresome correspondent with his 'strenuous recommendations' about trifling details, he must have found his tenant de Quincey doubly trying. De Quincey took the house in addition to Dove Cottage, which he continued to rent, but he was dilatory in paying his rent and then interminably procrastinated about leaving when Mrs Luff was anxious to move in and spend her final years close to the friends of her earlier days. She it was who vigorously set about improving and adding to the garden and grounds, the Wordsworths 'praising most sincerely her little plot of ground' when her energy and zeal began to flag. The Rydal

Mount household watched with keen interest the 'fresh proofs of her skill which appear almost daily'. When Dorothy declined in her later years, Fox Ghyll was often the limit of her walks, in what Mary described as her 'premature dotage'. At Loughrigg Holme nearby lived Edward Quillinan, who eventually took as his second wife Dora Wordsworth.

The house now called Stepping Stones, but formerly known as Spring Cottage, was the home of Dorothy Dixon, a great-granddaughter of William. It became the property of Willy, William's youngest son, and here Gordon Wordsworth arranged and annotated his grandfather's manuscripts.

The path this side of Pelter Bridge goes upstream to Rydalwater, along the shore of that lake and eventually onto Loughrigg Terrace with magnificent views over Grasmere.

Hacket is named on all the various popular editions of the Ordnance Survey maps and is close to the busy tourist routes, yet it remains almost a secret world, a peaceful island of quiet in the busy tourist area of Little Langdale.

In 1810 a cottage high on the fellside was the home of John Youdell and his wife Betty; their daughter Sarah was a maid at Allan Bank. All the Wordsworth children had been coughing and vomiting badly, and their doctor advised a change of air, at the Youdells' home. They could hardly have chosen a better spot. Dorothy was enchanted by the high situation of the cottage, commanding unfamiliar views of familiar fells: '. . . standing upon a hill overlooking Little Langdale, Tilberthwaite, Colwith, and the vale of Brathay; warm because it fronts the south, and sheltered by crags . . . at the door chuse to the right or to the left and you have mountains, hamlets, woods, cottages and rocks. . . .' She goes on to describe the 'heavenly' weather and how they sat outside in warm autumn sunshine while William read from *Paradise Lost*, and they looked down with wonder as they watched in the valley below 'a stream of white vapour' slowly ascending and melting away. The doctor's advice turned out to be sound, and they all returned home in better health.

While at Hacket, Dorothy was much alarmed when she lost her way one evening and had to seek help from a farm she stumbled across, having trudged almost blindly knee-deep through a peat bog. Today the 'trackless fields' which caused Dorothy to lose her sense of direction are strictly private.

A track does, however, lead to 'Iveing Howe', which is still pronounced 'Ivy How' by local Langdalians. This Ivy How is also of interest for its Wordsworthian associations, though to the democratic and egalitarian tastes of today the associations show him and his 'conspirators' in a rather dishonourable light. The story goes back to the Westmorland Parliamentary Election of 1818, when he was a vigorous supporter of the (Tory) Lowther cause – indeed his exertions on behalf of this faction seem to have precluded most other activities for many months. In the pre-reformed Parliament of the time, the vote went only to certain types of freeholders, and Wordsworth energetically organized a syndicate of eight friends and relatives (some of whom lived far away from the constituency) among whom smaller plots of the Ivy How Estate could be divided as a way of acquiring a vote. Naturally he ensured that all the men were staunch supporters of the Lowthers, who seemed to have had many friends in the Langdale area. To be fair to Wordsworth, the opposition party was resorting to similar tactics, and the whole situation demonstrates how pressing was the need for electoral reform.

On a walk through this quiet corner of Lakeland today, it is difficult to believe how fervent were the opposing sides and that this estate, now left in peace again, was at the centre of local political tactics. The only reminders are on the names shown on the present-day map, which echo the addresses and surnames of many freeholders whom Wordsworth canvassed: Walthwaite, Harry Place, Spedding Crag and Wyke Plantation.

Although his letters concentrate entirely on the political expediency of acquiring this estate, it is pleasing to note that Mary in one of her letters is more interested in the situation of the property: 'An hour ago a bargain was struck in this house for a beautiful freehold in Langdale ... a sweet sunny place with beautiful rocks. Yew trees and hollies. . . .' The trees around are still worthy of attention, the hollies and yews now less apparent, though, than the extensive coppiced woodland which cloaks the valley between the road and the river. A steep path descends to the beck and to Colwith Force, a waterfall that rarely disappoints as it forces its way through large boulders on its journey from Little Langdale Tarn into Elterwater.

This area had attracted Wordsworth's attention long before he became interested in the land merely as a means of securing the re-election of the Lowthers to Parliament. In his *Guide*, the force at Colwith is recommended, and he quotes lines of his own poem on Blea Tarn, a short distance away:

> A liquid pool that glittered in the sun,
> And one bare Dwelling; one Abode, no more!
> It seemed the home of poverty and toil,
> Though not of want: the little fields, made green
> By husbandry of many thrifty years,
> Paid cheerful tribute to the moorland House.

This passage and other fine descriptions of the area can be found in Book II of 'The Excursion', which includes the encounter with the Solitary, who hosts the poet and his companion at Blea Tarn House, which must be one of the highest inhabited houses in Lakeland, as well as one of the most beautifully situated. Today it is a farm guest-house, and Wordsworth would surely have approved of the present owners' reputation for good food and hospitality, since he too was simply but generously entertained there to a 'pastoral banquet' which included oaten bread, curd cheese, cream and 'whortle berries from the mountain side' as well as a 'small parade of garden fruits'.

At Blea Tarn on the longest day one may test Wordsworth's assertion that the sun sets between the two 'lusty peaks' of the Langdale Pikes:

> . . . there the sun himself,
> At the calm close of summer's longest day,
> Rests his substantial orb; – between those heights
> And on the top of either pinnacle,
> More keenly than elsewhere in night's blue vault,
> Sparkle the stars, as of their station proud.

Incidentally, the conifer trees and the rhododendrons were not to be seen when he wrote these lines in 'The Excursion', and in later editions of the *Guide* he adds a footnote to the effect that the 'quiet treeles nook' is 'No longer strictly applicable, on account of recent plantations'. In high summer, 'quiet' is 'no longer strictly applicable' either, on account of the widespread ownership of motor cars.

Great care is needed on the steep descent into Great Langdale, though the views are well worth a few raised hairs, but the narrowness of the road dictates that one parks at one or other of the two hotels near the valley head. Even from the car-park, it is obvious why this is one of the most popular spots for walkers and climbers in the Lake District. Unfortunately its popularity is so great that a good deal of work has been needed in recent years to prevent further footpath erosion. It is perhaps no longer a pleasure to walk up to Stickle Tarn, but for the energetic, with strong footwear and with a fine day, there is little danger of getting lost, as one will certainly not be alone and the well-worn tracks are as easy to follow as a major road.

The path above the New Hotel which goes by a seat and through a gate leads to the Dungeon Ghyll Force, referred to by Wordsworth in his poem 'The Idle Shepherd Boys'. This spectacular waterfall was a must for the nineteenth-century tourist, and the two hotels owe their existence to its reputation. Many visitors mistake Stickle Gill above the New Hotel for the Dungeon Ghyll, which, as the name suggests and as Wordsworth's poem tells, is in a deep ravine close by:

> The gulf is deep below:
> And, in a basin black and small,
> Receives a lofty waterfall.

Wordsworth asserts that, '. . . it cannot be found without a guide, who may be taken up at one of the cottages at the foot of the mountain,' and two recently published guide-books contradict each other, one telling the leader to look to the west of Mill Gill, the other to the right. However, a careful scrutiny of the large-scale OS map or a check in Book III of Wainwright's *Guide* will help to pinpoint it exactly.

Further down the valley, at Chapel Stile church, is the gravestone of Owen Lloyd with its inscription composed by Wordsworth. A mile and a half further south is Loughrigg Tarn which he praises in his *Guide*. It was a favourite place which always gave the family pleasure, described by Wordsworth as 'round, clear and bright as heaven'. Dorothy must have often visited the Tarn in later life and recalled the ecstasy with which she had once proudly ridden round the tiny lake on a pony which her brother Richard had given her. The combination of both rugged and pastoral scenery which so pleased her is still apparent.

5

Over the Raise

The Ancient Route between
Kendal and Keswick

The letters and journals of the Wordsworths and their friends are sprinkled with references to 'the Rays', as Dunmail Raise was then known. Strictly speaking, the Raise is the summit of the road between Grasmere and Keswick (the present A591), and it has always loomed large in the consciousness of Lakelanders. It once marked a national boundary, for to the north lay the ancient kingdom of Strathclyde. More recently it marked the boundary between the former counties of Cumberland and Westmorland. It is often a weather-divide, with sunshine on one side giving way to rain on the other. It was a route often followed by the Wordsworths, the Coleridges and the Southeys on their comings and goings between Grasmere and Keswick. They could walk it in just over four hours, and the unquenchable Coleridge might take in the top of Helvellyn as well. It is still a spectacular route, but in the days before tarmacadam and sophisticated highway engineering it could be arduous and dangerous as well. Not for nothing are there coaching inns on either side of the summit, strategically placed before the steep gradient begins. Not for nothing is one of the inns called 'The Travellers' Rest', though it might more appropriately have been named 'The Horse's Rest'.

Today experts say that there are 4.6 people in the population of England and Wales for every privately registered motor car. Planners calculate that – theoreti-

cally at least – around twenty million people live within
comfortable day-trip distance of the southern Lake District. If these figures seem unbelievable, stand by the busy
A591 and count well over one thousand cars an hour
passing by. If it was less busy in Wordsworth's day, the
road was no less important. Indeed, it was possibly more
important then, linking as it did the vital trade route
between Kendal and the flourishing West Cumberland
port of Whitehaven. This chapter will follow this route
from Kendal to Keswick and along the way look at the
many fascinating associations with the Wordsworths and
their friends.

Kendal in the early nineteenth century was a substantial
market town. It could even then make the proud boast that
it was mentioned in Shakespeare, or, more accurately,
that the woollen cloth known as Kendal Green which was
made in the town was referred to in *Henry IV, Part 1*.

   Throughout his adult life Wordsworth had cause to visit
the town regularly, on business or pleasure. In the period
leading up to the Westmorland election of 1818, when he
associated himself with the Tory Lowther cause, he seems
hardly ever to have been away from the town, busying
himself as an informer on the progress of the canvassing
and drumming up support for the Lowthers among his
friends and acquaintances. In his political lobbying and
advising he showed considerable knowledge of Kendal
folk and pragmatism. Knowing the Dissenters to be strong
in the town, he advised the Lowthers to change their motto
from 'Church and King' to 'King and Country' and, aware
of the Kendal tanners' pressure group, urged their support
for the repeal of the leather tax.

   The election was the first to be contested in Westmorland for over forty years and cost the Lowthers well over
£20,000. The constituency supported two members of Parliament and Lord Lonsdale fielded two of his sons, Lord
Lowther and Colonel Henry Lowther. Wordsworth frank-
ly admitted to Lord Lonsdale the disadvantage of both his
candidates being members of his family. Brougham, who
hoped to wrest one of the seats from the Lowthers, made

much of this nepotism in his campaign, supported by the *Kendal Chronicle*, the mouthpiece of the radical cause.

Aware of the handicap of not having such support on their side, Wordsworth urged successfully the formation of a newspaper which is still in existence today, the *Westmorland Gazette*. He also supported Thomas de Quincey as editor. But de Quincey, now resident at Dove Cottage, proved an exasperating choice and held the post but a short time. It must have given Wordsworth great pleasure to help found a rival to the radical *Chronicle*, which had left its readers in no doubt as to the identity of the meddlesome Lowther supporter, referred to by the paper as 'the Poetical Distributor of Stamps'. By this time Wordsworth had occupied the tax-collecting post of Distributor of Stamps for Westmorland for several years and the *Chronicle*'s contemptuous use of the qualifying adjective must have galled him. Bliss might it have been to be alive during the French Revolution, but for the older and, he would maintain, wiser Wordsworth, these must also have been heady days. His detractors make much of this so-called political apostasy, but it is likely that he was naturally a conservative and that his feelings in late adolescence were an aberration.

Nevertheless, his beliefs at this time put him in fear for his physical safety from the mob in Kendal, and after the election result was announced (a victory for the Lowthers), troops had to be called out to quell the disorder. Wordsworth also went in fear of losing his civil service post as Distributor of Stamps, since government employees were not supposed to indulge in direct political activity. Any spy stationed, for instance, outside Abbot Hall, the elegant riverside home of Christopher Wilson, a Lowther supporter, would have seen Wordsworth going and coming sufficiently regularly to raise eyebrows.

Kendal was also the home of the Cooksons, known as 'the Kendal Cooksons' to distinguish them from their relatives of the same name elsewhere. Sara Hutchinson (Mary Wordsworth's sister) had spent much of her childhood living with the Cooksons. Dorothy stayed from time

Ambleside: Wordsworth's Stamp Office

Wordsworth Memorial Window, Ambleside Church

Blea Tarn and The Langdale Pikes

Blea Tarn House

Poet's Seat,
Rydalwater

Dora's Field,
near Rydal
Church

Helvellyn

Skiddaw from Windebrowe

Greta Hall, Keswick

River Derwent

Cockermouth: William
and Dorothy's
birthplace (*above*); All
Saints Church (*left*)

Croglinwater

River Eden

Eusemere

Barton Church

to time at their Kendal home, much pleased with the company, but not always with the town. She described one visit as full of merriment: 'plenty of snuff . . . merry till twelve o'clock . . . the livliness does not extend to the town in general.' Incidentally Kendal is still one of the few towns in England which continues to manufacture snuff, and Dorothy was not only indulging a pleasure but also supporting a genuinely local industry. On another occasion with Elizabeth Cookson she made a criticism of towns which is still heard today when people are standing around waiting to be served in shops, or endlessly trailing around different streets; she writes: 'All towns are cold catching places for me.' In a happier mood she did walk along the canal bank as far as Natland Beck and also climbed Castle Hill. And at the age of forty-six she could justly boast of having walked from Rydal to Kendal on a cold and blustery day in less than five hours. But in later life she clearly found the town tedious and would never again, as she did in 1809, delight in spending a full twelve days here attending auctions and visiting shops in order to furnish Dove Cottage for de Quincey.

Wordsworth's Stamp Office duties took him to Kendal over many years, and he also banked with the Wakefield and Crewdson firms. Today only the nationally familiar banks are represented in the town, but the Crewdson and Wakefield families are still prominent in the business community. The *Westmorland Gazette* continues the tradition of guidebook publishing which has a long history in the town. The Kendal firm of Hudson & Nicholson was approached by Wordsworth in 1835 with a view to their publishing a new edition of the *Guide*. He rightly saw the advantage of using a local publisher who could ensure that the volume would 'circulate through the Lake District, and the leading towns of the North'. That same year he graciously accepted honorary membership of the newly formed Kendal Natural History and Scientific Society: such societies still flourish in the town. Any modern visitor or resident will see ample evidence that Kendal's advantages and disadvantages during the first half of the last century are still present today.

Just as today Kendal is an important centre for buses, so it was once a prominent centre for coaches. In 1839, for instance, Wordsworth rejoiced that his wife could travel from Loughborough to Kendal for less than £2, and he particularly admired the beautiful coach on the Kendal–Manchester route. Known as 'The Fair Trader', it was drawn by two horses in nine hours at a fare of 14 shillings on the inside or 10 shillings on the outside. An express coach today continues the service of linking Manchester with Kendal.

Wordsworth's part in the Westmorland election has shown that he was friendly with Christopher Wilson of Abbot Hall and visited him there. Wilson had been at Hawkshead Grammar School at the same time as Wordsworth, and so too had Thomas Holme Maude, another Kendal banker and former Mayor, who was at St John's, Cambridge, with him. So there were many personal, business and political reasons for his continuing connection with the town. Few of these seem to have inspired him to write any great poetry, though he did write an extempore elegy on hearing that the Vicar of Kendal had died in 1814.

One of the best ways of seeing the full glories of this historic route from Kendal to Keswick is to travel on the top deck of the double-decker bus which plies regularly between the two towns. Even Lakelanders who think they know the area intimately are astonished by how much more they see, being above the roadside trees, hedges and walls, where a quite extraordinary view of the passing landscape is possible. The pace of the bus too, though not exactly slow, allows more detail to be seen.

Climbing out of Kendal, the bus soon comes to an impressive sign marking an invisible but important boundary, unknown to Wordsworth but one he would have approved of: the boundary of the Lake District National Park. For conservationists, Wordsworth's greatest claim to fame is not his poetry but his statement in the *Guide* which is often taken as an anticipation of the day in 1951 when the Lake District was declared by Parliament Britain's largest National Park: '. . . the author will be joined by persons of pure taste throughout the whole island who, by their visits (often repeated) to the Lakes in the North of England, testify that they deem the district a sort of national property, in which every man has a right and interest who has an eye to perceive and a heart to enjoy. . . .' The rest of the journey will be entirely within the boundary of the National Park.

One further advantage of this bus route over others is the regularity in the summer of the buses – sometimes only half an hour apart, often an hour between them – so that in the summer passengers can get on and off to view places along the route. A first stop could be at the tiny hamlet of Ings, which straddles the main road just beyond Staveley. Here the schoolboy William and the adult Dorothy marvelled over the interior of St Anne's Church. William came over on the ferry as a schoolboy from Hawkshead specifically to see the famed Italian marble here and to learn the almost fairy-tale story of Robert or Richard Bateman who came from this parish from poor origins and made his fortune in the world of commerce overseas. Wordsworth's own lines have been engraved on a brass plate in the church and tell the tale:

> There's Robert Bateman, thought she to herself,
> He was a parish boy – at the church door
> They made a gathering for him, shillings, pence,
> And halfpennies, wherewith the neighbours bought
> A basket which they filled with pedlar's wares;
> And with this basket on his arm the lad
> Went up to London, found a master there,
> Who out of many, chose the trusty boy
> To go and overlook his merchandise,
> Beyond the seas; where he grew wondrous rich
> And left estates and monies to the poor,
> And at his birthplace built a chapel floored
> With marble which he sent from many lands.

The whole appearance of the church interior is reminiscent of the great City of London churches. It was built in 1743 and is a monument to Bateman, who never saw the completed building. The marbles are from Leghorn, though when Dorothy visited the church on her way back from the Yorkshire Dales in 1802, a local woman who showed her round insisted that they had been conveyed down the Red Sea. Dorothy was too good-natured to correct her, and in any case she was in high spirits that autumn on her stop at Ings, for she always relished this part of Westmorland, which gave her clear intimations that she was 'home': 'I am always glad to see Staveley it is a place I dearly love to think of – the first mountain village that I came to with William when we first began our pilgrimage together.' By the time she had reached Ings, she was fully refreshed, partly by a 'bason of milk' and partly by bathing her feet in the mountain stream, her solicitous brother insisting that she put back on her stockings, lest she catch a chill.

The almshouses close to Ings Church were also the work of Bateman, and if the church is locked, application should be made to the lady living in the house at the far end of the row.

The woman who showed Dorothy round the church also drew attention to the painting of the Last Supper, flanked by Moses and Aaron; the artist, she was told, had taken great pains to ensure that the details of the dress were faithful to the Biblical description. Another feature in the church worth inspecting is the painting of the building and the bridge which hangs by the door. This confirms Dorothy's own description that the church in her time was on the main coach route, whereas now it has been by-passed by a fast new road.

The two steep hills between Ings and Windermere slow the bus down considerably. The view from the second hill of a vast expanse of Lake Windermere is worth a longing, lingering glance, and on the left is the railway station – the terminus of the Kendal to Windermere Railway which Wordsworth strove so hard to prevent. But at least he could be pleased that it did not continue to Low Wood near Ambleside, nor on, as one adventurous scheme wished, by tunnel under Dunmail to Keswick. He feared that too many people arriving by train would spoil the peace of the Lake District, though he was keen enough to ensure that his own tourist guide was bought by visitors; as long as they had that eye to perceive and heart to enjoy, he was content.

In 1835 he published a sonnet in praise of 'Steamboats, viaducts, and railways', though his attack on railway mania is the poem more often quoted on the subject. This sonnet is entitled 'On the Projected Kendal and Windermere Railway' and has been used by modern conservationists as a kind of manifesto:

> Is then no nook of English ground secure
> From rash assault? Schemes of retirement sown
> In youth, and 'mid the busy world kept pure
> As when the earliest flowers of hope were blown,
> Must perish; – how can they this blight endure?
> And must he too the ruthless change bemoan
> Who scorns a false utilitarian lure
> 'Mid his paternal fields at random thrown?

But the rash assault on the insignificant hamlet of Birthwaite was made, and very soon the new town of Windermere, with its hotels and guest-houses, grew up. Almost immediately the Windermere railway became a fit subject for painters, and a recent exhibition at the Wordsworth Museum of paintings from the period 1810 to 1850 shows a puffing steam-train as seen from Orrest Head. But the Wordsworths did come to accept the railways sufficiently to make use of them when convenient. The speed was the great advantage, though Carlyle's description of a journey made in 1847 leaves one wondering whether the coach might have been preferable: '. . . nine hours of tempestuous deafening nightmare – like the hours of Jonah in the whale's belly'.

A mile or so beyond Windermere is the entrance to Calgarth Park, on the left of the road, home of Wordsworth's friend Dr Watson, Bishop of Llandaff. Another mile further on are the gates of Brockhole, the Lake District National Park Visitor Centre, where slide shows, lectures and day courses on Wordsworth and his contemporaries are held. After another mile there is Low Wood, an important coaching inn in the nineteenth century, now a centre for water sports, though its tradition of offering rest and refreshment for travellers continues.

Across the lake can be seen the turrets of Wray Castle, whose grounds are open to the public. It was built by an acquaintance of Wordsworth, and he, far from criticizing it, as one might have expected, maintained that the mock castle 'added a dignified feature to the interesting scenery in which it stands'. He planted a mulberry tree in the grounds.

Soon the bus comes into Ambleside, described elsewhere, and after another mile reaches the lane end which leads to Wordsworth's final home at Rydal Mount, the subject of another chapter. On the left, three hundred yards beyond the Glen Rothay Hotel, look out for the 'Poet's Seat' between the road and the shore of Rydalwater. Stone steps have been cut into this impressive outcrop of volcanic rock, and under the shade of the oak and ash lies one of Wordsworth's favourite musing spots, a cool place to picnic on a sultry summer's day.

Rydal Church and the adjoining 'rashfield' on the right-hand side of the road have rich associations with William and his family. The field is more often known as 'Dora's Field' and in early spring is a mass of golden daffodils. Originally intended as a site for a new house, it became a memorial to Wordsworth's daughter. Many people wrongly identify it as the place where he and Dorothy came across the famous daffodils in 1802. The church was built in 1824, and as early as 1822 there was mounting excitement in the Rydal Mount household at the prospect of a new chapel – and one so close to their home. Dorothy writes with emphatic excitement: '. . . the church *is* to be built – in the orchard adjoining our field', and so it was, on a site which Wordsworth helped to choose. It was their neighbour and 'landlady' Lady Flemming who endowed the building, which was finally consecrated on Christmas Day 1824.

Dorothy gave a stone-by-stone commentary on the progress of the building work, writing in the autumn of 1823: 'Our church is near finished on the outside is very pretty &

you can have no idea how beautiful in connexion with the
village, especially seen from the other side of the lake.'
Later it gave her constant pleasure, when illness confined
her to her room at the Mount, to look from her window:
'How pretty the chapel tower looks from my bedroom . . .
and how charming the prospect.' It cost Lady Flemming
£1,500, and she installed as curate a distant relative,
Fletcher Flemming, the son of Hawkshead schoolfriend
John Flemming of Rayrigg. Imagine the Wordsworth's
pride and pleasure when their eldest son, John, now
ordained, preached in the chapel in the spring of 1828.
Naturally Wordsworth found this a fit subject for a poem
addressed to Lady Flemming, 'On seeing the foundation
preparing for the erection of Rydal Chapel, Westmoreland':

> How fondly will the woods embrace
> This daughter of thy pious care,
> Lifting her front with modest grace
> To make a fair recess more fair. . . .

This was written in 1823, and in the following year he
must have re-read these lines with a certain irony, for he
described graphically a devastating whirlwind that
attacked some of the trees here: 'In one quarter you might
imagine that giants had been hurling Oaks and Pines at
each other after tearing them up by the roots. . . . Sixty
trees have been overthrown, and out of 15 hundred the
greater part show vestiges of this tornado, which raged
with its utmost fury into the Cove of Rydal.' Wordsworth
hated to see a single tree felled, let alone witness this kind
of destruction. There is a reference to his love of trees on an
engraved brass plate which has been fixed to a rock deep in
these woods. The lines are his, and he would have delighted in the notion of their being read here, 150 years after
his rescue operation.

> In these fair vales hath many a tree
> At Wordsworth's suit been spared;
> And from the builder's hand this Stone,
> For some rude beauty of its own,
> Was rescued by the Bard;

So let it rest; and time will come
When here the tender-hearted
May heave a gentle sigh for him,
As one of the departed.

The nearby Glen Rothay Hotel incorporates what was known to the Wordsworths as Ivy Cottage or Tillbrooke's Cottage. It belonged for a time to the Reverend Samuel Tillbrooke of Peterhouse, Cambridge, and when he was not resident, he was happy to let it out. William's brother Christopher stayed there when George Canning visited Rydal Mount and William's future brother-in-law, Edward Quillinan. In 1827 the Bishop of Chester rented the house for a family holiday lasting several months. In the same year Dorothy complains that it was 'absolutely *cased* in ivy . . . transformed into a *green box*', and when eight years later a Mr William Ball bought the property and greatly enlarged it into its present size and renamed it Glen Rothay, Wordsworth sardonically dubbed it 'the Botched Ivy Cottage'.

At the foot of the Rydal Mount hill is Spring Cottage, where the Arnolds stayed in 1831, cementing their friendship with the Rydal Mount household. The Arnolds brought eight children with them, transforming the quiet hamlet for the duration of their six-week stay. On another occasion the Wilberforces paid an extended visit, taking with their large family and retainers every available space in the hamlet.

When the celebrated portrait-painter Pickersgill was arranging a visit to Rydal, Wordsworth recommended him to take the early coach from Kendal to arrive at Rydal, advising him to travel on the outside for the sake of the view. The equivalent advice today for the next stretch of road is to travel on the bus's top deck, for the views across Rydalwater are superb. Continuing their Dove Cottage pastime of rowing out to Grasmere Island, the Words-worths made Rydalwater's islands also a favourite destination for a rowing excursion. This revived an earlier association with the lake, for during their first year at Grasmere they had rowed out to one of the islands to give

Wordsworth the opportunity of composing one of his inscriptions with a highly detailed title: 'Written with a slate pencil upon a stone, the largest of a heap lying near a deserted quarry, upon one of the islands at Rydal'. The poem tells the story of Sir William Flemming's intention to build a summerhouse here, but on being informed that the lake was shallow enough for a man to wade out and take possession of the house and declare himself a freeman of the isle,

> . . . the prudent Knight
> Desisted, and the quarry and the mound
> Are monuments of his unfinished task.

Finally Wordsworth in verse warns off any future developer, urging them to leave

> Thy fragments to the bramble and the rose;
> There let the vernal slow-worm sun himself,
> And let the redbreast hop from stone to stone.

Usually in the summer the lake is calm, but in the *Guide* there is an account of a particularly dramatic storm on 30 March 1822 when 'an eddying wind scooped the waters out of the basin, and forced them upwards in the shape of an Icelandic Geyser, or boiling fountain, to the height of several hundred feet.'

On the right-hand side of the lake is the whitewashed Nab Cottage, now a guest-house, occupied by de Quincey in 1829, the home then of his father-in-law, John Simpson. Years before, de Quincey had courted Margaret Simpson here, and she bore him a son before they eventually married. Hartley Coleridge, son of Samuel Taylor, also lived here. Above the storm porch a black diamond-shaped stone has the distinctive date 1702. The road formerly went right beside the cottage door and is now the private drive.

At White Moss Common the bus continues to Grasmere along a road built after the Wordsworths had left Dove Cottage. The more energetic traveller might prefer to alight from the bus and take the narrow, steeply rising road which strikes off to the right. This eventually rejoins the A591 just beyond Dove Cottage. There are fine views to be enjoyed from this route, and part of it is covered by an interesting cassette tape which can be hired from Dove Cottage for those who enjoy hearing, rather than reading, about the literary associations. Among the landmarks pointed out is the coffin stone where coffins were rested on their way to their final resting-place in the churchyard. There is also the site of the Wishing Gate, referred to by Dorothy in her Journal as 'Sara's Gate'. In a note to the poem inspired by this gate, Wordsworth explains the origin of the name 'from a belief that wishes formed or indulged there have a favourable issue':

> Smile if thou wilt, but not in scorn,
> If some, by ceaseless pains outworn,
> Here crave an easier lot;
> If some have thirsted to renew
> A broken vow, or bind a true,
> With firmer, holier knot.

After the gate was destroyed, he wrote some verses lamenting its destruction, only to learn later that he had been misinformed and to find on a visit to the spot his 'old favourite unmolested'.

On the opposite side of the road is 'John's Grove', often mentioned by William and Dorothy and a favourite resort of their brother John. It became to them a sacred place after he was drowned. The wood between this and the main road is known as Bainriggs and was likewise beloved by the family. Here Wordsworth frequently composed poetry during his years at Dove Cottage.

The visitor can rejoin the bus at the point where the White Moss road meets the major road, or can view Dove Cottage, the church and the village of Grasmere, all of which are the subject of other chapters. The bus winds through the village before rejoining the main road half a mile north of Dove Cottage opposite the Swan Hotel. From now on 'The Waggoner' will be an almost constant companion during the 'long ascent of Dunmail Raise'. On the inn sign to the Swan Hotel is a line from the poem 'Who does not know the famous swan', the rustic lay of the hapless Benjamin. It was on this stretch of road between the hotel and the summit that the inevitable misfortunes began to overtake the good-natured and kind-hearted Waggoner and his asses. The skies darken and large raindrops are followed by peals of thunder and flashes of lightning.

On the left can be seen the distinctive-shaped rocks on Helm Crag, known as 'the Lion and the Lamb', or as 'the Lady at the Organ', depending on your imagination. Wordsworth sees the rocks as representing an astrologer at his desk with an old woman:

> Dread pair that, spite of wind and weather,
> Sit still upon the crag together.

On the opposite side of the road, behind the Swan Hotel, Greenhead Gill tumbles down to swell the River Rothay as it rushes towards Grasmere. A brisk walk up the ravine leads to the ruins of what is thought to have been 'Michael's Sheepfold' (not visible from the road). It makes a fine evening walk for visitors staying in Grasmere, especially in the heat of summer when the frothing pools make ideal bathing spots. The serenity and grandeur of this place on a summer's evening are at variance with Wordsworth's wistful poem of the son who failed to live up to his parents' high expectations. Perhaps one can imagine that the larger stone was the very one laid by Michael's son Luke as the first stone of the fold, before leaving home never to return. For many, Michael's ghost haunts the sheepfold he never finished – symbol of his disappointment and dejection. The cottage where he lived has gone, and great changes have apparently taken place in the neighbourhood:

> . . . yet the oak is left
> That grew beside their door; and the remains
> Of the unfinished Sheepfold may be seen
> Beside the boisterous brook of Greenhead Ghyll.

There are sombre thoughts a little further along the road over the Raise, for just north of the Traveller's Rest inn a packhorse route signposted 'Helvellyn Patterdale' goes via Grisedale Tarn, where Wordsworth said his fond farewell to his brother John in 1800; in 1805 he drowned when the ship he captained was wrecked off the Dorset coast. On the Patterdale side of the Tarn, where the path to Helvellyn branches off, an engraved plate marks the spot of this 'Brothers' Parting'. The verses Wordsworth inscribed on a rock here have vanished.

As the road continues its climb, two farms can be seen on the right – the first is Broadrain Farm and a little further on High Broadrain. Here lived the Reverend Joseph Sympson, Vicar of Wythburn, described by Wordsworth as 'the Patriarch of the Dale' and who at eighty was an active mountain walker who astonished Dorothy by his ability to fish the high tarns. The broad fell to the right is Seat Sandal, 'fond lover of the clouds'.

At the summit of Dunmail (that is, at the 'Raise'), there is a heap of stones, now islanded by the dual carriageway. Here is the former divide between Cumberland and Westmorland; here was the boundary between England and the ancient Kingdom of Strathclyde; and here is the site of a great battle between the Norse King Dunmail and the Anglo-Saxon King Edmund of Northumbria. The tradition that Dunmail was slain and buried here persists, and that the heap of stones marks his grave. In fact he died in Rome a good many years after the battle here in AD 945. Wordsworth is probably partly responsible for continuing the tradition:

> . . . that pile of stones,
> Heaped over brave King Dunmail's bones,
> He who had once supreme command,
> Last king of rocky Cumberland;
> His bones, and those of all his Power,
> Slain here in a disastrous hour.

The summit is a favourite alighting point from the bus for walkers anxious to scale the heights with a minimum of uphill slog, for the Raise is nearly eight hundred feet above sea-level. It was a ruse Dorothy recommended to

friends and visitors intent on climbing Helvellyn. In 1828,
for instance, she advised a correspondent to choose a
Wednesday, Friday or Monday for the attempt on the
mountain, those days being the ones when the coach to
Keswick allowed passengers to alight at the summit.

The contrast between the weather to the north and that
to the south of the Raise is often remarked upon by locals
and visitors to the Lake District. Dorothy, in 1801, returning to Grasmere after a stay in Keswick, comments on the
contrast between the landscape she had left behind 'fresh,
green and beautiful', and the appearance of her home vale,
which was 'miserable . . . burnt as brown as an autumn
stubble field'. Of course the contrast can easily operate in
the opposite way, and the weather on and around the
summit is usually breezy and occasionally fierce. One such
day occurred in December 1833 when Edith Southey with
her fiancé and his sister were returning home to Keswick
after staying at Rydal Mount. Their post-chaise and
horses were blown to the very edge of the precipice, and
they crawled and clung to boulders and walls for four
miles, their muffs, combs and similar items being whipped
out of sight by the ferocious wind. But when Wordsworth
was away from the Lake District and saw a beautiful
sunset – less common in the Lakeland hills than elsewhere – it often brought to his mind the grand sunsets he
had seen over the Raise.

The descent down the north side of the Raise is rapid,
and as the road levels out, there are traces of the more
ancient route on the right, where a bridge and a track can
be seen about twenty yards away from the present road. At
the roadside a stone plaque set into the wall reads:

> 30th of NMO 1843
> Fallen from his fellows side
> The steed beneath is lying
> Harnessed here he died
> His only fault was dying
>   WB

A further stone below this reads, 'This stone was re-
erected on this site by the Manchester Corporation Water-

works Committee 1948.' A quarter of a mile further on, by the telephone kiosk, is a slab of stone five feet high which appears at first to be a tombstone. In fact, it is a handsome tribute to Wordsworth's friend Matthew Arnold, as the inscription tells: 'A record of the two walks from hence over the Armboth Fells July 1833–43 which inspired Matthew Arnold's poem "RESIGNATION" and in reverent memory of the poet born 24th December 1822, died 15th April 1888.' There follows a quotation from the poem which will appeal to all fell-walkers

> We left us ten years since you say
> That wayside inn left today
> And now behold in front outspread
> Those upper regions we must tread
> Mild hollows and clear heathy swells
> The cheerful silence of the fells
>
> MA

Close by is the church of Wythburn, which has been described as being now rather like a stranded boat without an ocean to sail on or a crew, and few other places in any tour of the Wordsworth Country require greater flights of imagination in order to recreate the scene so familiar to the Wordsworths and their friends. The flooding of the area by Manchester Corporation at the end of the nineteenth century has wrought great changes, and the immediate area around the church is now among the most sparsely populated regions in the Lake District, considering its proximity to a major road. The crowded gravestones in the churchyard are the first indication of the parish's former life. Today there are only occasional services in the summer, and the enlarged car-park at the rear is now a popular place for motorists to abandon their cars for the three-hour foot-slog to the top of Helvellyn. Few people linger around the church; most are in transit, by car or on foot.

Not so, however, in Wordsworth's time, for here was a flourishing and warm-hearted community, renowned for generous hospitality. Immediately opposite the church on the other side of the road was an inn, the 'Nag's Head', and north of this was another public house, the 'Cherry Tree'. Today both have been demolished. Inside the church is an old photograph of the 'Nag's Head' with bold lettering announcing on the gable end of the rough cast building, 'Bainbridge's Nags Head INN, luncheons and teas'. In 1829 Dorothy referred to the fame of the inn, a welcome harbour for travellers, who must have been hard pressed to decide whether to refresh here or at the nearby 'Cherry Tree', equally hospitable and the setting for the 'Merry Night' described in 'The Waggoner'.

Although today there is no inn to tempt one to stop, the church is certainly worth a visit. The present building dates from 1640, although there was a chapel here in 1554. It is characteristic of many Lakeland churches in the remoter parishes, a simple building with thick stone walls liberally whitewashed and with stone flags on the floor, which in this case slopes noticeably in line with the slope of the hillside into which it is set. It is easy to discern the Victorian additions.

Not far from this spot, Wordsworth organized a celebrated picnic attended by Mary, Dorothy, Sara Hutchinson, his brother John and Samuel Taylor Coleridge. The site they chose was Black Crag, by the older road which went along the east shore of the lake, which in those days was of course much lower than the present reservoir. And here they commemorated their happy sojourn by carving their names on a rock, thereafter known to as 'the Rock of Names'. In the manuscript version of 'The Waggoner' is a passage about the rock which was withheld from the early published version of the poem; it now makes poignant reading:

> . . . they were graven on thy smooth breast
> By hands of those my soul loved best;
> Meek women, men as true as true and brave
> As ever went to a hopeful grave:
> Their hands and mine, when side by side
> With kindred zeal and mutual pride,
> We worked until the Initials took
> Shapes that defied a scornful look. . . .

When the level of the lake was raised, the engineers tried to rescue the rock to present it to the Wordsworth Institute in Cockermouth. But the rock crumbled, and all that was possible was to rescue the parts with the names on and build them into a cairn-like structure which was placed above the present road one fifth of a mile north of the straining well (disguised as a mock baronial-style castle). In 1984 the rock was in urgent need of conservation and Michael Berry, Managing Director of English Lakes Hotels, sponsored its restoration and removal to Dove Cottage.

Bearing in mind the later history of this rock seems to add an extra relevance to another of Wordsworth's poems on this area. The setting is a little further north, near the village of Legburthwaite, and the poem is called 'Rural Architecture'. Just north of the 'King's Head' at Thirlspot and on the opposite side of the road is 'a single and conspicuous hill' called Great How. The poem tells the charming story of childhood perseverance, concerning 'three rosy-cheeked school-boys' who climbed to the top of the hill and built from the stones thereabouts the shape of a man, which was so large in proportion to the diminutive size of the boys that the locals dubbed it 'The Magog of Legberthwaite Vale'. When the wind demolished their efforts a few days later, they returned and built another, and Wordsworth holds them up as an example to revive his spirits on occasions when they are inclined to flag.

What with Rock of Names, the Magog of Legburthwaite and the large cairn at the summit of Dunmail Raise, this area seems to have had more than its fair share of stones. But the most impressive stones are still ahead, at Castlerigg, the site of a neolithic stone circle. Although it can be approached by car from the Keswick–Penrith road, one might leave a car or alight from the bus on the A591 one mile north of the telephone kiosk and layby at Dale Bottom. The lane which leads to the circle is just one mile south of Keswick, and although a car can be driven along here, it is not advisable, being a very narrow way with few passing-places. In any case it makes a most easy walk with very fine views. A sign at the junction of the main road reads 'Castlerigg Stone Circle' but can easily be missed on the drive up the brow of the steep hill on the way to Keswick. The strip of tarmac ensures that the way can be followed without difficulty in any weather, and within minutes the walker is unaware of the busy, noisy road left behind. This is an ideal gentle introduction for companions who are reluctant to walk or for children unused to walking or even for pushing a pram or wheelchair along. The advantage of this approach soon becomes obvious as the panorama of hills opens on all sides. Choose the mid-morning when the sun is behind you, and you are in for a special treat: ahead to the left is the mighty bulk of Skiddaw; ahead to the right is the wonderful Blencathra Range, well justifying from this angle the alternative name of Saddleback, with its highly distinctive profile. To the right is a very extensive, almost complete, view of the Helvellyn Range, with the odd conical-shaped tip of Mell Fell just peeping up over Clough Head, and away in the distance the Pennines. The lane affords glimpses of small areas of Bassenthwaite Lake and Derwentwater and the flat and level 'interlaken' area which now separates the two stretches of water which in post-glacial times would have formed one large lake.

The lane follows the summit ridge of the small but detached hill on which the circle has been built, and this accounts for the extensive views that can be enjoyed with so little effort. There is ample scope for blackberrying at the right time of the year, and during the late summer the heather on the slopes of Blencathra and Skiddaw is a sight to behold, and photograph.

Looking back, the heads of some of Lakeland's shapeliest summits jockey for attention: the long ridge which begins with Catbells and continues to Maiden Moor, Eel Crags and on to Honister Hause; the ridges which culminate in the tops of Causey Pike and Grisedale Pike. These are the mountains of 'All shapes and sizes' which Coleridge so admired when he settled at Greta Hall.

Still there is no indication that one of Lakeland's most impressive historical sights is near. Ahead and slightly to the right is a well-constructed stone barn, and beyond this field the stone wall gives way to a high hawthorn hedge. At the junction of wall and hedge a stile gives access to the field of the stone circle, impressively glimpsed from the platform of the stile, forcing itself on the attention and surprising even the most accurate of map-readers who might have already anticipated its location. The lichens which bespatter the stones must have been present throughout most of its long history. When Wordsworth and Coleridge came here in 1799, they found that vandals from Keswick had whitewashed the circle. Although in the eighteenth and nineteenth centuries the circle is consistently referred to as druidical, it is much older than the Celtic period, older indeed than the more famous Stonehenge. Nobody could fail to be astonished by both the construction and situation of this ancient relic. Curiously Wordsworth in his *Guide* does not specifically mention Castlerigg, though he devotes a long passage and some verse on circles generally, and comments on an even less popular circle, Long Meg and her daughters, which can be seen at Little Salkeld, beyond Penrith.

The view to the south-east of the Helvellyn range is spectacular. Of all the high peaks of Lakeland, it is Helvellyn which Wordsworth and his friends climbed most often. The famous portrait of him aged seventy by Benjamin Haydon is fancifully set on the summit, which he climbed that year. In 1805 he climbed the mountain with Walter Scott and Humphry Davy, and in 1817 he climbed it twice within a three-week period, once with Mary and once with Dorothy. The previous year Dorothy and William, returning from a stay at Hallsteads, Ullswater, took in Helvellyn from the Patterdale side. It was one of those early summer days when the mountain air is almost intoxicating: 'I never walked with more spirit in my life, than on the lofty terrace of Helvellyn,' wrote Dorothy. Looking back down on the tiny houses, Wordsworth sees the contrast between the freedom of the hills and the restrictions of daily life:

> . . . that man could e'er be tied
> In anxious bondage to such nice array
> And formal fellowship of petty things!

Both Wordsworth and Scott were much moved by the story of one Charles Gough, an artist, who fell to his death near Red Tarn in April 1805 and whose terrier bitch guarded her master's corpse until it was discovered a full three months later. By then the terrier was semi-wild and had given birth to a litter of puppies. The two poems were apparently produced quite independently. Wordsworth's captures the other worldness of the high fells as he looks down on Red Tarn, which is everything one expects of a mountain lake:

> There sometimes doth a leaping fish
> Send through the tarn a lonely cheer;
> The crags repeat the raven's croak,
> In symphony austere;
> Thither the rainbow comes – the cloud –
> And mists that spread the flying shroud;
> And sunbeams; and the sounding blast,
> That if it could, would hurry past;
> But that enormous barrier holds it fast.

Wordsworth especially admired Scott's lines addressed to the dog:

How long did thou think that his silence was slumber?
When the wind waved his garment how oft didst thou start?

6

'By Skiddaw's Lofty Height'

Keswick, Borrowdale and Derwentwater

Although Keswick has expanded considerably during the twentieth century, there is still a great deal in the town and the surrounding area to absorb the visitor's interest. In his *Guide* Wordsworth tells of an early association with the locality: 'In my youth, I lived some time in the Vale of Keswick, under the roof of a shrewd and sensible woman, who more than once exclaimed in my hearing, "Bless me! folk are always talking about prospects: when I was young there was never sic a thing neamed."' But hers was the last generation to disregard 'prospects', or views as we should say today, and the high street of the town, where almost every shop tempts the visitor to buy a colour postcard, is clinching evidence that a picturesque view still has a powerful attraction. But stunning though many of the views are in this area, it was personal friends which brought the Wordsworths so frequently to the town. Indeed, it was here that Dorothy and William were able to live together under the same roof in their beloved Lakeland after years of separation, when their kind and generous friend Raisley Calvert arranged for them to stay at his brother William's house, called Windebrowe, sometimes referred to as Windy Brow.

Set under the flanks of Latrigg, the house is now owned by the Calvert Trust, which arranges outdoor adventure holidays for the disabled. The Trust have furnished two rooms, known as the Wordsworth Rooms, which are open to the public at certain times and are also opened by arrangement for groups. Here William and Dorothy were blissfully happy at being together again, though they were obliged to live frugally in order to keep within their very modest income. In a letter written in 1794 from Windebrowe, Dorothy describes their austere diet: '. . . our breakfast and supper are of milk and our dinner chiefly of potatoes and we drink no tea. . . .' But despite these privations they enjoyed the company of the Speddings of Armathwaite and of the Calverts when they were at home. They enjoyed too the magnificent view which they could obtain by climbing onto a natural terrace on the side of Latrigg, a little way above the house, where they could see what Dorothy described as '. . . a huge pile of grand mountains in whose lap the lovely lake of Derwent is placed . . .'.

Old Windebrowe is approached from Keswick along Station Street, turning right at the junction opposite the Fitzpark Museum (where, incidentally, there is a good display of Lakes Poets' manuscripts). The road goes by the side of the grounds of the Keswick Hotel until on the right a sign marks a junction to 'Windebrowe and Brundholme – Road unsuitable for vehicles after ½ mile'. Pedestrians can cut through the park by the bowling-greens and then walk along the pleasant road to Windebrowe which commands unexpectedly fine views of Latrigg, Skiddaw, Catbells and Walla Crag. The lane is lined in places with hedges of hawthorn and beech, and the fields on either side are peppered with fine trees – oak, horse chestnut, limes. Unfortunately a new fast road cuts Latrigg off from the Windebrowe lane, but one can still appreciate why Dorothy found the area so exquisitely beautiful.

Although the farmhouse had undergone a number of changes by the time the Calverts sold it to the Speddings in 1833, the building is essentially one of the oldest in the Keswick area. It dates back to the sixteenth century, when it was occupied by German miners from Augsburg who came to Cumberland to work the forge at nearby Brigham. Although William and Dorothy's stay was but a few months – they left in May 1794 – William returned in the June to nurse the ailing Raisley Calvert, dying of consumption. Calvert died in January 1795, with Wordsworth still ministering to him, an act of devotion which Calvert rewarded with a bequest of £900. It was this money which eventually enabled William and Dorothy to set up house together at Dove Cottage.

The two 'Wordsworth Rooms' open to the public are full of interest. The simple furnishings and the stone floors and thick walls recall the 1790s, helped by a carefully selected range of exhibits. On the walls are engravings by the Reverend Joseph Wilkinson, whose artistry was much derided by Wordsworth after he had written his original *Guide to the Lakes* as an accompaniment to Wilkinson's drawings. A poem Wordsworth had published in the *Morning Post* in 1800 was written here. The piece is signed with the pseudonym 'Ventfrons' – Latin, literally, for 'Windy brow'. It rejoices in one of those detailed titles in which Wordsworth wallowed: 'Inscription for a seat by a roadside halfway up a steep hill facing south'. It begins:

> Thou who in youthful vigour rich and light,
> With youthful thoughts doth need no rest,
> Oh thou to whom alike the valley and the hill
> Present a path of ease . . .

— an appropriate sentiment today since the farm is now used as an adventure centre for the disabled.

The Keswick bypass cuts off Latrigg from the farm, but in the 1790s of course William and Dorothy had direct access onto the hill.

To the north-west of Latrigg a terrace road leads to the hamlet of Applethwaite, where in 1803 Wordsworth was presented with a small cottage by Sir George Beaumont. Beaumont's generosity was prompted by his admiration of both Wordsworth and Coleridge, and he felt that, if they lived closer together, their work would be mutually enriched. The property is still called 'The Ghyll' and remained in the Wordsworth family for many years after William's death. However, the wish of Beaumont remained unfulfilled, namely that the two poets should use the cottage 'To communicate more frequently your sensations to each other', and Wordsworth never actually lived there. He did, however, greatly admire this part of the Keswick area, and Applethwaite had long been a favourite subject for painters. In Dove Cottage Beaumont's own drawing of Applethwaite Dell had pride of place by the Wordsworths' fireside. In 1819, writing to Lord Lonsdale, he urged him to direct the visiting Prince Leopold along the Applethwaite road to admire the views here and at the nearby hamlet of Ormathwaite.

An easy stroll along the terrace road and short paths in this area is always rewarding, and one path passes in front of Ormathwaite Hall, which some Wordsworth scholars persist in confusing with Armathwaite Hall at the north end of Bassenthwaite Lake. Both halls have associations with William and Dorothy, but Dorothy's detailed description of Ormathwaite Hall places it accurately. She was writing in 1810 to a friend who was thinking of purchasing the property, so she certainly took good care to be accurate. Today the house, viewed from the path, is still faithful to her letter: '. . . the imagination cannot conceive a more delightful place, and that the house is placed just in the very spot where it ought to be . . . a pretty low white house . . . and immediately above rises Skiddaw.'

Skiddaw Mountain had many associations for the Wordsworths and their friends, some of them stretching back to their earliest years. It was distant Skiddaw which benignly presided over the young William's play during his early years at Cockermouth

> . . . when crag and hill,
> The woods, and distant Skiddaw's lofty height,
> Were bronzed with a deep radiance. . . .

And in their later years it continued to loom large, literally and metaphorically, in the family's experience. A memorable occasion occurred on Skiddaw in 1815 when on 21 August the victory of Waterloo was celebrated on the summit of the mountain – which had long been one of the chain of beacons which enabled warnings to be transmitted to distant counties. No doubt this made the idea of a Waterloo bonfire all the more appealing to the group of worthies who gathered together as night fell. Among the company which Robert Southey so vividly described were William, Mary, their son John (aged twelve), James Boswell (son of Dr Johnson's biographer), Lord and Lady Sunderlin and sundry other notables, as well as a few tourists and some rowdy Keswickians. Southey's own description sets the scene: 'We roasted beef and boiled plum puddings there; sung "God save the King" round the most furious body of flaming tar barrels that I ever saw; drank a huge wooden bowl of punch; fired a cannon at every health with three times three, and rolled large balls of tow and turpentine down the steep side of the mountain. The effect was grand beyond imagination. . . .'

Despite these extraordinary hazards only one mishap occurred, and that involved Wordsworth, who apparently accidentally knocked over the kettle of boiling water which had been brought to dilute the punch. He tried to hide his offence, but a sharp-eyed lady ('the Senhora') identified him beyond dispute as he was wearing Edith Southey's red cloak. Southey perceived that Wordsworth was unaware that his misdemeanour was known and quietly went round the company telling them of the crime. They all conspired to surround him and broke out in an accusatory and teasing chant, ''Twas *you* that kicked the kettle down! 'Twas you, Sir, you!' This little contretemps, however, led to the Waterloo celebrations developing into a most hazardous evening in which the participants were lucky to return home unscathed. The loss of the punch water meant that all the available surface water on Skiddaw was used by Southey's party, and the rabble from Keswick were obliged to drink their own supplies of rum neat. The enthusiasm for the celebration thus gathered apace: 'All our torches were lit at once by this mad company, and our way down the hill was marked by a track of fire from flambeaux dropping the pitch, tarred ropes etc. One fellow was so drunk that his companions placed him upon a horse, with his face to the tail, to bring him down, themselves being just sober enough to guide and hold him on.'

Today, Skiddaw is still occasionally used for celebrations and beacon lightings – on Queen Elizabeth's Silver Jubilee for instance. But they are much more sober affairs, carefully governed by the Society of Civil Engineers' guidelines for safe beacon firings. Old Skiddaw survives them all.

The great centre of activity for the Wordsworths in the Keswick area was Greta Hall. Now part of Keswick School, and open only by advance arrangement, the Hall attracted Samuel Taylor Coleridge in the first summer of the nineteenth century, and Robert Southey, who came here to live in 1803. Today the view has been somewhat marred by more recent industrial and residential development, but imagination can reconstruct the stunning effect the surrounding countryside had on the occupants and their guests. Coleridge left in 1803, but Robert Southey and his family lived there until his death in 1843. Southey's wife and Coleridge's wife were sisters, and their respective families continued to live together at Greta Hall for many years – during which Coleridge made only infrequent visits. The Wordsworths had, during Coleridge's time at Greta Hall, been regular visitors – William and Dorothy stayed over a week there within a month of Coleridge's first arriving. The habit continued long after Coleridge began his restless wanderings.

With such panoramic views to distract the occupants, it is astonishing that so much was written here – especially by Southey, whose library became justly celebrated, eventually containing over fourteen thousand books, collected over many years and genuinely cherished. How painful it must have been for the mild-mannered Southey to have to observe Wordsworth molesting his books. It was said that he was not beyond opening uncut pages of a new book with a buttered knife, and Southey asserted that to introduce him into a library was like letting a bear into a tulip garden.

Today the Hall is kept in excellent state of repair but, tucked away behind the main school buildings and barely glimpsed except from near the adjoining pencil factory, it seems to have conspired with the surrounding flourishing trees to hide its past from the world. However, it has an interesting connection with Wordsworth's poem about Benjamin the Waggoner, for the builder of Greta Hall (William Jackson) was none other than Benjamin's master.

A short distance to the north-west is another building with close associations with the Wordsworth Circle, and also one of the most ancient sites in the area. Crosthwaite Church, despite the expansion of Keswick, still manages to preside in much of the splendid isolation it enjoyed in the early nineteenth century. Set on the outskirts of the town, it is surrounded still by pleasant fields with open views of the surrounding hills. Along the path to the church came the families of Wordsworth, Coleridge and Southey, to baptisms and weddings, funerals and thanksgivings. Coleridge's children (Hartley, Derwent and Sara) were christened at the church, after which they had a grand feast of a roast pig from Eusemere. Sara Coleridge married her cousin Henry Nelson Coleridge here, with Wordsworth's eldest son John officiating and his daughter Dora and three of the Southey children among the eight bridesmaids. In 1843 Wordsworth and his son-in-law Edward Quillinan attended Southey's funeral here, and Wordsworth's inscription on the tomb in the chancel can be read today:

> Sacred to the memory of
>   Robert Southey,
> Whose mortal remains are interred
>   in the adjoining churchyard.
> He was born at Bristol, August xii,
>   m.dcc.lxxiv and died
> after a residence of nearly xl years,
> at Greta Hall, in this Parish,
>   March xxi, m.dccc.xliii.
> This memorial was erected
> by the friends of Robert Southey.

It must surely have been the intention of his friends to erect a memorial to the graceful, benevolent and charming man such as would speak across the years of the affection in which he was held. And in this they have certainly succeeded. The altar tomb is surmounted by the reclining figure of Southey and was said to be a good likeness. The effigy of the Poet Laureate, book in hand, was the work of an inspired self-taught sculptor, Lough of Newcastle. It was originally intended that the stone should be Caen, but the sculptor substituted white marble at his own expense. The memorial verses on the tomb are also Wordsworth's. These eighteen lines were carefully composed and were subjected to at least one revision. They conclude with a fitting reference to the 'local' mountain which they both so loved:

> His joys, his griefs, have vanished like a cloud
> From Skiddaw's top; but he to heaven was vowed
> Through a life long and pure; and christian faith
> Calmed in his soul the fear of change and death.

Local people are still apt to refer to Derwentwater as 'Keswick Lake', and the town has staunchly insisted in its publicity and entrance signs that it is not simply Keswick but 'Keswick on Derwentwater'. And who can blame them, for has not Derwentwater been, from the dawn of tourism in the area, 'Queen of the Lakes'? For many *aficionados* it is *the* lake for sheer beauty and variety. In his *Guide* Wordsworth singled out this lake for particular praise and maintained that it most nearly approached perfection due to its shape, which least resembled a river and therefore most nearly conformed to his ideal of what a lake should be like. In correspondence with prospective visitors to the Lake District, he shows a detailed familiarity with Derwentwater and Borrowdale. He was fascinated by the so-called floating islands which periodically appear and then mysteriously disappear again at the southern end of the lake. He urged Lord Lonsdale to ensure that Prince Leopold travelled on the west side of the lake on returning to Keswick from Borrowdale: still excellent advice today for those who wish to enjoy almost aerial views from the comfort of their cars.

There are four islands on Derwentwater. The one in the middle of the lake – St Herbert's Island – is said to have been the hermitage of the saint. He was a disciple of St Cuthbert of Holy Island and so admired him that he wished to die at the same time as Cuthbert. According to tradition, this wish was granted and the two saints died on the same day. The island became a place of pilgrimage, and Wordsworth, inspired by the story as well as by the surrounding beauty, wrote a twenty-seven-line inscription, 'For the spot where the Hermitage Stood on St Herbert's Island, Derwent-water', imaginatively reconstructing the hermit's cell:

> . . . behold this shapeless heap of stones,
> The desolate ruins of St Herbert's Cell.
> Here stood his threshold; here was spread the roof
> That sheltered him. . . .

However, by the time Wordsworth came to write his *Guide*, he was less enthusiastic about the island, complaining that the venerable wood which for centuries had sheltered the hermitage had been felled and replaced by 'spindly Scotch firs'. His objection was not simply visual – though his eyes were pained by the sight of conifers, even the lovely larch: his objection was also on historical grounds, since he could no longer indulge in the pleasing fancy that the oaks might have descended from the very ones planted by the saint thirteen hundred years ago.

Wordsworth also condemned the work on another island by an 'alien improver'. The culprit was a gentleman from Nottinghamshire rejoicing in the name of Joseph Pocklington, and on some old maps and engravings the island is shown as 'Pocklington's Island'. It has also been known as 'Vicar's Island' and on more recent maps as 'Derwent Isle'. It was indeed an eccentric extravaganza which included a druid temple, a whitewashed Gothic structure which 'reared its august head in all the pride of pasteboard antiquity', and sundry other theatrical pieces. How Wordsworth lamented the appearance of such monstrosities and the demolition of such rustic features as the sycamore-embowered cattleshed.

Friar's Crag, a short walk along the shore from the boat landings, was so called because of its associations with pilgrims embarking on visits to St Herbert's Isle. It has long been one of the most famous beauty spots in Lakeland, and vies with Tarn Hows and Ashness Bridge for the accolade of the most photographed view in the region. It has become so popular that the National Trust has been obliged to fence off parts of the area to allow regeneration of the vegetation, worn down by millions of feet. Wordsworth recommended the view from here, and a monument records that John Ruskin came as a very young child with his nurse: it was, he said, his first memory, and the effect of that view upon him remained in his mind all his life. It held a similar fascination for Wordsworth, and in 1841, detained in Keswick on business, he walked back and forth along the shore here for well over two hours, musing and composing.

In the St Herbert poem, Wordsworth refers to the cataract of Lodore, which was an almost compulsory stop for the correct tourist throughout the nineteenth century. On Peter Crosthwaite's map of 1809 it is referred to as 'The great Water fall', by the hotel whose name was then spelt 'Low Door'. The owner of the present Swiss Hotel is still happy for visitors to view the falls (on hotel land) which are approached through one of those curious turnstiles more often seen in football stadiums. A 5p coin is the modest admission charge. If there has been dry weather in the preceding weeks, the falls can be nothing more than an impressive collection of mossy boulders, bereft of water. But see them after a spell of heavy rain and they are unforgettable, living up to Southey's much anthologized poem addressed to his children on 'How does the Water Come down at Lodore'. Southey takes well over two hundred lines to answer the question – lines which, if read aloud with the gusto they demand, leave the reader literally as well as metaphorically breathless. No poet has ever so enjoyed himself with such sustained onomatopoeia and rhyme:

> Rising and leaping,
> Sinking and creeping,
> Swelling and sweeping,
> Showering and springing,
> Flying and flinging,
> Writhing and ringing,
> Eddying and whisking,
> Spouting and frisking,
> Turning and twisting. . . .

Two and a half miles further along the road in to Borrowdale, beyond the hamlet of Grange, is another famed spot beloved of the picturesque tourist – the Bowder Stone, a vast boulder of volcanic rock which appears to balance precariously on the ground but which has remained there for possibly thousands of years. Wordsworth insisted that Prince Leopold should see this curiosity. Even those visitors who had time only to circumnavigate Derwentwater were urged by Wordsworth to abandon their circuit for a short distance in order to marvel at this phenomenon.

The yew trees celebrated by Wordsworth's poem have disappeared from Derwentwater and Borrowdale, though that ancient and noble species is still well represented in the valley. His 'fraternal four' yews were just above the road from Seatoller to Seathwaite and are shown in a drawing made in 1883, just before the first of them to be destroyed was uprooted in a gale. Impressed as he was with the solitary Lorton Yew, he was even more taken by the Borrowdale trees:

> Joined in one solemn and capacious grove;
> Huge trunks! and each particular trunk a growth
> Of intertwisted fibres serpentine
> Up-coiling and inveterately convolved . . .
> To lie, and listen to the mountain flood
> Murmuring from Glaramara's inmost caves.

A painting hangs in the Wordsworth Rooms at Old Windebrowe to give a visual illustration of his poem.

To the north of Derwentwater is Bassenthwaite Lake, which Wordsworth in his *Guide* says should be circumnavigated. He and Coleridge had stayed a night in an inn at Ouse Bridge at the northern tip of the lake. The inn has long gone, but the view from Ouse Bridge of the 'bright blue river' of Wordsworth's youth can still be seen. Was it while admiring the view with Wordsworth from the bridge that Coleridge resolved to call any future child he had 'Derwent' in homage to this spot?

Armathwaite Hall nearby is now a hotel – and a very stately one indeed. The original Hall, which Wordsworth knew when it was occupied variously by the Speddings and Sir Frederick Vane, has been demolished. But at Mirehouse on the eastern shore of the lake is one of the most recently opened literary properties. Here lived James Spedding, the great Baconian scholar. Tennyson, Fitzgerald and Carlyle all visited the house. Wordsworth had been at Hawkshead Grammar School with two of the Speddings, then living at Armathwaite Hall. He had probably met Tennyson at Cambridge, and when Tennyson stayed at Mirehouse, he called on Wordsworth at Rydal Mount. The house has much to interest Wordsworthians, including some fine portraits and landscapes.

7

'Much Favoured in my Birthplace'

Cockermouth, Lorton and North Cumbria

At the age of twenty-three Dorothy Wordsworth revisited the house in Cockermouth where she and her brothers had been born. It was not a happy occasion for her as she found that, '. . . all was in ruin, the terrace walk buried and choked up with the old privet hedge which had formerly been most beautiful, roses and privet intermingled – the same hedge where the sparrows were used to build their nests. . . .' If she could return today, she would be delighted, for the house is now cared for by the National Trust, having been bought in 1937 by public subscription when the property was in danger of being demolished to make way for the town's bus station. The bulldozers and excavators will not be allowed a second chance, and the Cockermouth buses have had to be content with a less historic site.

The house where the Wordsworths were born was then, and is still now, the most imposing and elegant house in the town. It was completed in 1745 for one Joshua Lucock, Sheriff of Cumberland, and was acquired by the Lowthers a few years later. It remained in the hands of the Lowther family until 1885, and as early as 1896 there were moves to secure the property as a national monument.

It might seem that Wordsworth, born into a wealthy and splendid environment at Cockermouth, must have fallen on bad times during his early adult life, since he was obliged to live in such cramped quarters at Dove Cottage.

The truth is that he never actually owned any of the houses in which he lived. The birthplace was provided for his father by Sir James Lowther, for whom John Wordsworth worked as an estate and law agent. There is no record in his meticulously kept accounts of any rent having been paid, so presumably the house 'went with the job'.

William was born here on 7 April 1770. His elder brother, Richard, had been born two years before; three more children were to follow: Dorothy, born on Christmas Day 1771, John in 1772 and Christopher in 1774. Several passages in 'The Prelude' testify to the delight the boy William took in his surroundings. He was, by his own admission, 'much favoured' in his birthplace, and he reserved a special delight for the River Derwent, 'the fairest of all rivers' which had 'blended with his nurse's song'. His life-long fondness for what today's countryside planners refer to somewhat pompously as 'water-borne recreation' must surely date from this very early period. Throughout his life he never lost his love of rowing, ice skating and viewing lakes, rivers and waterfalls. And it was here that it all began:

> Oh! many a time have I, a five years' Child,
> A naked Boy, in one delightful Rill,
> A little Mill-race sever'd from his stream,
> Made one long bathing of a summer's day,
> Bask'd in the sun, and plunged, and bask'd again. . . .

There are still to be seen in the town many former mill buildings with their races, and none more appropriate in this context than the so-called Double Mills on the banks of the River Cocker to the south of the town. This mill has been imaginatively converted into a fine youth hostel so that, over two hundred years on, youngsters can still enjoy the delights that Wordsworth made so famous. But 'Cocker' is by far from being the most poetic name for a river, and it is the 'Derwent' which Wordsworth mentions in his poems, and the 'Derwent' after which Samuel Taylor Coleridge named one of his sons – wisely perhaps, despite the more alliterative claim of 'Cocker Coleridge'.

The garden of the birthplace is a delight, and from here one can still hear the river which blended with William's nurse's song and admire the plants which have been carefully selected by the Gardening Adviser to the National Trust, so as to consist only of specimens mentioned by the Wordsworths or which are known to have been typical of the time the family lived here. Any more recently produced hybrids are firmly excluded, however attractive, in the interests of historical accuracy. The walled garden at any time of the opening season is worth lingering in, and brings visitors back to admire the changes. In the spring, daffodils and snowdrops are in evidence; later the celandine, and later still the herbaceous borders are magnificent.

The garden is not seen from the outside of the house, hidden by high walls and by the imposing Georgian façade of the building from the front. An excellent view of the house can be had opposite the front entrance on the other side of the road, where a bust of Wordsworth mounted on a plinth is a memorial provided by Cockermouth's Rotary, Round Table and Lions Clubs. It was unveiled on the two-hundredth anniversary of the poet's birth by Colonel J. G. Wordsworth. From this vantage-point the house presents a confident face to the busy world rushing by on the road immediately in front. Self-assured and secure behind the distinctive gates with high piers on either side, the visitor is left in no doubt that Sheriff Lucock built his house to reinforce his own ideas of self-importance. The entrance is up a flight of steps and through a doorway sheltered by a porch with Doric columns.

At the entrance, a guide greets visitors and gives an introduction, before leaving them to view the house. The dining-room is immediately to the right, and here prints and paintings decorate the walls, including a series of prints of Lakeland views dated 1810, by the Reverend Joseph Wilkinson, the very prints for which Wordsworth originally wrote his *Guide*. On publication, however, he greatly disapproved of the quality of these illustrations, which were omitted from the later editions which he himself supervised. Looking at them today, however, one must be grateful to the Reverend Wilkinson, for it was his illustrations which gave birth to a *Guide* which is still one of the most popular introductions to the Lake District. Had Wilkinson not invited Wordsworth to write a topographical text as a 'foil' to his engravings, there might have been no *Guide*, which, for many people, was Wordsworth's greatest claim to fame in his own lifetime. Indeed, Matthew Arnold reported that a naïve clergyman had once enquired of him whether Wordsworth had written anything *apart* from his *Guide to the Lakes*.

In addition to the changing display of prints and paintings in this room is a fine 1816 Broadwood piano, which is regularly played, often while visitors are viewing the house and occasionally for evening recitals. Here too, evening lectures and special events are held from time to time, and wine and cheese served. These evening gatherings provide an excellent opportunity to experience the atmosphere of the house as it must have been in the days when it was fully lived in. On such occasions one can really appreciate Pevsner's perceptive description of the building as 'quite a swagger house for a town of this size'.

The morning room on the other side of the entrance hall is much smaller and contains contemporary panelling. The Crown Derby tureen, plates and dish are part of a service which belonged to Wordsworth. On the walls are portraits of him and those of many of his distinguished friends and contemporaries.

Upstairs, the first room off the landing is the study, and by the study the reading-room. Here there are local newspapers set out as well as a national newspaper for the day, and a collection of books. From the window there is an even finer view of the garden. An interesting print shows the former Moot Hall of Cockermouth with its curious outside staircase and three-arched arcade.

At the front of the house, with blinds to protect the furnishings from the afternoon sun, is the drawing-room. Usually over the fireplace hangs Turner's painting of Kilgarren Castle.

The bedroom contains a four-poster, a rocking cradle and an oak chest, and along the corridor is a room which is devoted to a display of local crafts, where there are regular craft demonstrations held during the season.

Downstairs again, the old kitchen and housekeeper's room have been tastefully converted into a coffee shop which is fast becoming famous for the home-made fare which is served here: local Cumberland farm cheeses, Border Tart and gingerbread are just some of the delicacies available, and lunch can be accompanied by a glass of the National Trust's own wine. Down a further flight of stairs is a door which gives access to the walled garden, a fitting climax to a tour of the house. The exit is via a stone-flagged laundry, a room which contains an excellent exhibition about the work of the National Trust in the Lake District and where there is an audio-visual presentation available throughout the day. Beyond this is the National Trust shop, which fronts onto the high street of the town.

On leaving the shop, two right turns around the outside walls of the house lead to the riverside walk which gives views of the castle and of the confluence of the rivers Cocker and Derwent. Although the castle is no longer open on a regular basis to the general public, it is still open on specified days during the Cockermouth Festival in August. It is the home of the Dowager Lady Egremont, and the structure we see today dates mostly from the fourteenth century, although there has been a fortification on this site since 1134. Here in the grounds of the castle and on the battlements the young Wordsworths loved to play, and William, looking back on those halcyon days in his early sixties, could still vividly recall the excitement, the joy and also the fear, which add greatly to all youngsters' games. In 'Address From the Spirit of Cockermouth Castle' written in 1833, he imagines the spirit of the ancient pile addressing the aged poet:

> . . . when thou in boyish play,
> Entering my dungeon didst become a prey
> To soul-appalling darkness. Not a blink

Of light was there; – and thus did I, thy Tutor,
Make thy young thoughts acquainted with the grave;
While thou wert chasing the winged butterfly
Through my green courts; or climbing, a bold suitor,
Up to the flowers whose golden progeny
Still round my shattered brow in beauty wave.

The other building in the town to visit is the church, where both Dorothy and William were baptized – and on the same day. But for the bravery of officials who dashed into the blazing building and rescued the registers when the church was burned down in 1850, the tangible proof of this would have been lost. The building the Wordsworths knew was in fact a chapel of ease attached to the church of Brigham, two miles downstream of the River Derwent, where, by a curious coincidence, William's son John would one day be the vicar. And John's son (also John) would succeed his father there.

The present church is built on the strong foundations of this chapel, which was described by travellers as a pleasant building a hundred feet long and forty-five feet wide with galleries on both sides. The minister in their time was the Reverend Joseph Gillbanks, who was also master of the grammar school which the children attended. Inside the church are two items of particular interest. To the left of the altar is a brass wall plaque inscribed: 'To the Glory of God and the honoured memory of William Wordsworth Poet Laureate the east window of this Church is raised in this his native place by public subscription AD MDCCCLM.' Close by is a wooden plaque with gilt lettering and the arms of the Lowther family, with whose fortunes the Wordsworths' own were closely intertwined. The plaque records the generosity of the Earl of Lonsdale in giving property yielding £100 a year to support an assistant curate.

One of the town's traditions, recalled by Wordsworth, concerned the public catechizing of All Saints Sunday School pupils. They filed ceremoniously from the school building and into the church, with the churchwardens and sidesmen at the head of the procession, the bells chiming and the children dressed appropriately:

From Little down to Least, in due degree,
Around the Pastor, each in new-wrought vest,
Each with a vernal posy at his breast,
We stood a trembling, earnest company!
With low soft murmur, like a distant bee,
Some spake, by thought-perplexing fears betrayed;
And some a bold unerring answer made.

This ceremony seems to have been better organized than the proceedings in the Grammar School, which Wordsworth also attended. Years later he compared the Cockermouth institution quite unfavourably with his Hawkshead School, where he said he learnt 'more of Latin in a fortnight than I had learnt during two preceding years . . .'.

One of his few memories of his mother was of her pinning a nosegay to his breast before he entered All Saints Church to say the catechism. He also recalled a woman doing penance in the church, dressed in a white sheet. He was disappointed, though, that he had not been given the penny he had been promised for witnessing the event, and confessed as much to his mother. 'If that was your motive,' she retorted, 'then you were very properly disappointed.' Perhaps, in his sixty-sixth year, Wordsworth recalled this incident and allowed it to spur him on to yet greater efforts to raise money for the building of an additional church in the town: 'My arm aches with scrawling letters about my poor church,' he wrote.

In the churchyard, a plain headstone marks the grave of William's father, John, with the inscription, 'To the Memory of John Wordsworth who departed this life 30th December 1783 aged 42 years.' Attending one's father's funeral must be quite one of the most dispiriting ways of beginning a new year, and Wordsworth recalled later a curious and ancient custom in Cockermouth: 'No funeral,' he said, 'took place without a basin of boxwood being placed in front of the house from which the coffin was taken up, and each person who attended the funeral took a sprig from it and threw it on the grave.' The children were now orphans, their mother having died five years before, and this marked the end of the Wordsworth connection with the town for many years. Thus for the Wordsworth children Cockermouth would always be associated with the time in their young lives when they were uniquely together as a family. When, almost exactly half a century later, William's first granddaughter was born and soon after his son's family moved to Brigham just two miles downstream from his birthplace, it was with peculiar pleasure that he contemplated the baby Jane 'gathering pebbles' and 'culling flowers' among his own haunts of so many years before.

His son John, once appointed to the living at Brigham Church, set about building a vicarage a few hundred yards to the east of the church in a field which in those days went straight down to the banks of the river. Today a fast road separates the house from the riverside, and the vicarage has been sold and is now a private dwelling. The design of the house suggests it might have been based on a child's conception of what a house should be like: a door centrally placed, with a window either side on the ground floor. On the first floor, windows match those below. But then a variation which no child and few architects would think of: instead of a chimney at either gable end, there is a cross at each end, and the chimneys are set a little way in. The view from the field must have been obscured by plantings in more recent years, for Wordsworth, when the house was being built, wrote of the site '. . . commanding beautiful views up and down river, with Cockermouth Castle in the middle distance, and Skiddaw in the background'.

But if the view was idyllic, life within these four walls was not always so content. John was often despondent about the prospect of a reformed Parliament taking away his living and encouraging further the already strongly radical and dissenting atmosphere of the Cockermouth area. Furthermore, when his wife's wealthy family fell upon hard times, they found that their income of £180 a year was hardly enough. At one time they considered taking in private pupils for tuition, but such pupils were not immediately forthcoming, and his father wrote to a friend in Ireland to see if two boys could be found whose parents would pay 'quite handsomely' for board and education, adding that 'Parents in the south seem to have an unaccountable objection to sending their sons to the north.' If these troubles were not enough to cope with, John suffered from typhus, as a result of ministering to a parishioner.

Even as the foundations for John's new home were being laid, William was moved to address an encouraging sonnet to him, entitled 'To a Friend – On the Banks of the Derwent':

> Pastor and Patriot! – at whose bidding rise
> These modest walls, amid a flock that need,
> For one who comes to watch them and to feed,
> A fixed Abode – keep down presageful sighs . . .
>> A welcome sacrifice
> Dost Thou prepare, whose sign will be the smoke
> Of thy new hearth. . . .

But if there was dissatisfaction with the parishioners, there can have been no dissatisfaction with the church building itself. Despite the proximity today of a busy highway, the church still conveys a rustic peace. It is usually locked, but helpful caretakers at the village post office and general store some half a mile away are happy to allow interested visitors a key.

There were several holy wells around here, and the 'Nun's Well' referred to by Wordsworth in his sonnet was close to the vicarage:

> The cattle crowding round this beverage clear
> To slake their thirst, with reckless hoofs have trod
> The encircling turf into a barren clod;
> Through which the waters creep, then disappear,
> Born to be lost in Derwent flowing near. . . .

A convenient scenic excursion may be made from the Cockermouth area by travelling south through the Vale of Lorton and along the shores of two of the least spoilt lakes – Buttermere and Crummockwater. A short diversion will also take in Loweswater. Because of the relative remoteness of this part of the Lake District, the Wordsworths seem to have visited it less frequently. But when they did walk in this area, they were always enthusiastic about the scenery.

An undeservedly neglected corner of Lakeland, the Vale of Lorton has a charm all of its own, and every guidebook which mentions the Vale almost always mentions the yew tree which Wordsworth made famous in his poem beginning 'Pride of Lorton Vale'. This magnificent tree is at High Lorton but can easily be missed on these winding lanes. Look out for a fingerpost directing to 'Boon Beck Scales' and cross the narrow bridge at this point. In a field beyond the telephone kiosk is the enormous tree with shapely, almost sculptured, branches stretching right across the beck and almost touching the house on the opposite bank. (Not surprisingly this house is named Yew Tree View, and the converted mill, now the village hall, is known as Yew Tree Hall.) The trunk of the tree is gnarled and pitted and twisted into the most fantastic shapes, and a circle of dry stone walling has been built around the base of its trunk, as if to give it extra dignity in its old age. The girth must be some thirteen feet, and the branches from tip to tip must extend to at least forty-five feet. Dorothy records visiting this 'patriarch of yew trees' with William in 1804, and his poem is ecstatic:

> There is a yew tree, pride of Lorton Vale
> Which to this day stands single in the midst
> Of its own darkness as it stood of yore . . .
> Of vast circumference and gloom profound
> This solitary tree! a living thing
> Produced too slowly ever to decay;
> Of form and aspect too magnificent
> To be destroyed. . . .

A few miles further south, at Scale Hill, Loweswater, Dorothy later admired more recently planted trees, which their friends the Marshalls had introduced. At Scale Hill was the 'roomy inn, with very good accommodation' recommended by Wordsworth, and where today the tradition of good food and hospitality is kept up.

Inevitably the 'Wordsworth Country' is thought of as synonymous with the Lake District, but there is another fascinating tract of land, not quite Lakeland, not quite 'the Border Country'. It lies to the north of a line drawn, say, from Cockermouth to Penrith and stretches up to and around the county town of Carlisle. Here are many quiet, unregarded backwaters which the Wordsworths either passed through *en route* to Scotland or Carlisle or visited on business or to call on friends.

Sometimes these spots give unexpected perspectives on the Lake District to the south and the Scottish hills to the north, as at Plumbland Church, two miles south of Aspatria. Here Wordsworth came to visit a friend in 1841 and must surely have been impressed with the view. He was certainly impressed with the church and comments on the exceeding beauty of the arch. Although much restored in 1870, the church still has many ancient features to marvel over. One of the windows shows Sir Edward Stanley, with shield and sword, whose family William's son John married into.

William's younger son, Willy, became Sub-Distributor of Stamps in Carlisle, and so the family visited there frequently. They also had brief encounters with the city in their comings and goings between the Lakes and Scotland. On a visit to Walter Scott at Abbotsford in 1831, William and Dora must have cut odd figures as their carriage entered the city, for a child exclaimed, 'There's a man wi' a veil, and a lass drivin'.' The veil was to protect Wordsworth's acutely sensitive eyes from the light during one of his recurring eye complaints. Two years later he attended the Assizes, where Lord Lonsdale was prosecuting several newspapers for libel, and played a small part in the trial as Distributor of Stamps, staying on to see the proceedings, which resulted in the prosecution of the proprietor of the radical *Carlisle Journal*.

It irritated Wordsworth to contemplate the fact that he had never sold a single copy of his poems through any Cumberland bookshop, but at least these later visits left better impressions than one of their earliest visits with Coleridge in 1803. Then they complained that their walk along the city walls was spoilt by the fact that the stone was in parts crumbling away and marred by 'disgusting filth'. Today Carlisle is proud of its history and is rapidly becoming a most admired historic city, with its impressive castle, several first-rate museums and, the city's pride and joy, the cathedral.

The great natural feature of this part of Cumbria is the River Eden, along whose banks Wordsworth wandered in a transport of delight. Discovering these nearby beauties relatively late in life forced him to contemplate that ever-present irony of travel – the neglect of fine things close to home in the restless urge to see far-off wonders. He sees some comfort in having in his sixties gained some intimate acquaintance with a river which he had formerly only glimpsed and mentioned in his poetry but once:

> But I have traced thee on thy winding way
> With pleasure sometimes by this thought restrained –
> For things far off we toil, while many a good
> Not sought, because too near, is never gained.

Surprisingly, perhaps, in view of his early opposition to the railways, a monument to that age also inspires a sonnet. The poem is entitled 'Steamboats, Viaducts and Railways', and his note makes it clear that he was impressed with the two viaducts which had been built near Wetheral and Corby.

Further upstream at Nunnery he rejoices in one of the Eden's tributaries – Croglinwater. It can best be viewed in the grounds of the house called the Nunnery, famous locally for the beautiful walks on the estate. The path from the house is immediately enjoyable: there are stately trees, including an exceptionally fine beech, around the red sandstone house, and the way is lined with red campion and pleasantly contrasting leafy sections and open fields. The rich red-coloured soil leaves no doubt about the geology of this area. Through the first kissing-gate there is a first glimpse of Croglinwater, in a calm, slow, gentle mood, and a remarkable contrast in the space of a few dozen yards, where the stream is transformed by a series of cliffs into a boiling cauldron of a waterfall. This contrast features in Wordsworth's sonnet:

> He raves, or through some moody passage creeps
> Plotting new mischief – out again he leaps
> Into broad light, and sends through regions airy,
> That voice which soothed the nuns while on the steeps
> They knelt in prayer, or sang to blissful Mary. . . .

The Nunnery paths are clearly waymarked, and a map board gives a choice of three walks of varying length. In former times there were usable footbridges across the ravine, but these are clearly dangerous and are now closed. If the object is to see the waterfall as soon as possible, the recommended walk should be reversed. This way one comes very soon to some steep steps with wooden handrails which lead to the fall itself. The roar of the water as it cascades into the pool below the cliff is so loud as to make speech practically inaudible. The force of the fall hitting the pool is so strong that spray is sent over six feet into the air. Spindly mountain ash cling to rock ledges, and ferns precariously decorate the rockface. It is without doubt one of the most dramatic natural sights in Cumbria.

For readers with a genealogical interest in the Wordsworths, a visit to the church at Lazonby is recommended. A former vicar was William's uncle the Reverend Thomas Myers. He died at the age of ninety-three and was buried here in 1826. There is a memorial to him in the stone floor of the chancel.

South of Lazonby, along an unclassified road near Little Salkeld, is a prehistoric monument which Wordsworth had known since early childhood, though he visited it for the first time only in 1821. An occupational hazard for all travellers is the risk of visiting a celebrated spot only to find that it fails to live up to expectations: not so with this ancient monument, known as 'Long Meg and her daughters'. The evocative name excites high expectations, which Wordsworth found amply fulfilled as he came 'suddenly and unexpectedly' on these standing stones. The poem the sight inspired is expressive of that sense we experience when confronted by man-made monuments built thousands of years ago and still tantalizing as to their precise origin and purpose. Even though there are good signposts to the site, it still comes as a surprise to find this curious arrangement of stones in such a remote and unfrequented place. Long Meg herself is the tallest of the stones and is set apart from most of the other stones which form the monument. If they are largely in their original positions, they must have been placed with great deliberation and strong (if now unfathomable) purpose. A vague and ill-defined sense of wonder and speculation fell on Wordsworth when he was faced with such puzzling evidence of prehistoric society:

> A weight of awe, not easy to be borne,
> Fell suddenly on my Spirit – cast
> From the dread bosom of the unknown past,
> When first I saw the family forlorn.
> Speak Thou, whose massy strength and stature scorn
> The power of years. . . .

Three miles north of Greystoke is Hutton in the Forest, home of Lord Inglewood and open to the public several days a week in the summer. In 1799 Wordsworth refers to the 'great library' belonging to Sir Frederick Fletcher Vane of Hutton and Armathwaite. Indeed, he urged Coleridge to settle in the north specifically to make use of the fine collection of books owned by Vane. Although modern maps persist in emblazoning the words 'Inglewood Forest' over a wide expanse to the north of Hutton, this area is today characterized by attractive open farmland rather than by dense tree cover. The medieval Forest of Inglewood stretched for fifteen miles south from Carlisle to beyond Hutton, which was one of the most southerly manors. When Wordsworth penned his sonnet 'Suggested by a View from an Eminence in Inglewood Forest' in 1831, the forest was even then no more than a distant folk memory – hence the opening lines:

The forest huge of ancient Caledon
Is but a name, no more is Inglewood,
That swept from hill to hill, from flood to flood. . . .

Nevertheless, there is still a sense of entering a special and different area 'behind' the Lakeland hills and towards Hutton.

In the grounds of Hutton are some fine specimen trees, and the terraced formal gardens around the house are graced by topiary and neat lawns. The setting is an idyllic foil for a fascinating house which happily blends the styles of at least three different periods: the medieval pele tower; the Jacobean and Baroque central portion and a tasteful Victorian wing, suggesting respectively a fairy-tale castle, an Oxford college and the mansion of an eminent Victorian. Wordsworth stayed here in 1836 and became quite friendly with the Fletcher-Vanes, who stayed at Rydal Mount. Their friendship probably stemmed from their mutual admiration for Lord Lonsdale and is another instance of the increasingly exalted circles in which the poet moved in his later life.

8

The Earth-embracing Sea

The Cumbrian Coast, the River Duddon and the Western Dales

Although few twentieth-century holiday-makers visit Cumbria for its coastal and seaside features, in the seventeenth, eighteenth and nineteenth centuries consciousness of the sea was much more common than it is today. Before the railway age and for over thirty years after Wordsworth's *Guide to the Lakes* was written in 1810, the most usual way to enter the region was by coach through Lancaster to Hest Bank, then across the Sands at low tide. Even with the dawn of the railway age and the beginnings of tourism as we know it today, sea travel played an important part in people's journeys. Before the Furness Railway was completed in 1846, a tourist from London could take a train from Euston Station direct to Fleetwood on the Lancashire coast and then transfer to a steamer for a sail across Morecambe Bay to Bardsea on the Furness promontory. From 1847 the steamer sailed into Barrow to connect with the newly constructed railway. Thus, whichever of these routes was chosen, the tourist approached the area via Furness, where Wordsworth had spent happy days as a child and as an undergraduate.

Furness Abbey in particular made a singular impression upon him, and descriptions of this monument to the piety and skill of the Middle Ages recur in his letters and poems throughout his life. In his *Guide* he recommends readers who 'are not afraid of crossing the Sands' to view these 'celebrated ruins', and this almost on the very first

143

page of his book. This is fitting, for it seems that among his first excursions to any historical monument after he had left his family home to attend the Hawkshead school was his outing to Furness Abbey. In 'The Prelude' he tells of how one of the highlights of his time at Hawkshead was the (rare) extravagance of hiring a 'galloping steed' and making for Furness – an intention he had to hide from the inn-keeper who hired out the horses, for the distance of over twenty miles he knew was 'too distant far For any cautious man'. So there was the unusual excitement of a long day's riding to a romantic and historic destination, spiced additionally for the mischievous schoolboy by the need to deceive the inn-keeper. The end justified the means, as the excited and ecstatic description in 'The Prelude' shows.

Since Wordsworth's death, a major Cumbrian town, Barrow in Furness, has spread out almost to embrace the grounds of the abbey itself. Almost, but not quite, for one of the most astonishing contrasts of modern Cumbria is that between the peace and 'other worldness' to be found among these sandstone ruins and the bustling town which has mushroomed up almost in the last hundred years. The abbey ruins and the immediate grounds are now in the care of the Department of the Environment, and there is the usual and ubiquitous custodian, in his recently completed 'visitor centre', where an excellent exhibition interprets the life and times of the abbey and its inhabitants. The schoolboy William found no custodian, no printed booklets and no visitor centre, but what he found then we can still find today:

> . . . the antique Walls
> Of that large Abbey which within the Vale
> Of Nightshade, to St Mary's honour built,
> Stands yet, a mouldering Pile, with fractured Arch,
> Belfry, and Images of living Trees,
> A holy Scene!

At the age of seventy-four, when his days of galloping down to Furness in an 'uncouth race' were long over, he

Brougham Castle

Lowther Castle

Countess' Pillar, near Penrith (*left*)

Furness Abbey (*below*)

Piel (Peele) Island

Black Combe

Whitehaven

Moresby Church

Birks Bridge, River Duddon

St Bees Head

Stepping-stones, River Duddon

Side Farm, Ullswater, and the field 'as level as a bowling green' (*below left*)

The Kirk Stone (*above*)

Wordsworth Cottage, Patterdale (*below right*)

Gowbarrow,
Ullswater (*above*)

Park House (*left*)

took up his pen and wrote a stinging letter to the *Morning Post* berating the entrepreneurs intent on building a railway line from Kendal to Windermere. Furness Abbey received an honourable mention in this letter in a passage which shows Wordsworth not as a writer of sublime and elevated verse (in which guise he is well known) but in the convincing style of a trenchant ironist, an effective style rarely seen in his poetry: 'Upon good authority I have been told that there was lately an intention of driving one of these pests, as they are likely too often to prove, through a part of the magnificent ruins of Furness Abbey – an outrage which was prevented by someone pointing out how easily a deviation might be made; and the hint produced its due effect on the engineer.' This long letter and an even longer sequel are now printed as an appendix to the Oxford University Press edition of the *Guide*. Present-day conservationists will find that his comments strike many familiar chords.

Even in its ruined state, the abbey really is a most impressive monument. The transepts and choir are almost their original height, and the great east window is awe-inspiring in its dimensions. But not only are the vastness and scale of the architecture a source of wonder: the detailed carving which survives is also a joy to behold.

Standing awestruck in the nave, the young William was transported by the sound of a 'single wren' which

> Sang so sweetly mid the gloom . . .
> . . . that there I could have made
> My dwelling-place, and lived for ever there
> To hear such music. . . .

In addition to these extracts from 'The Prelude' and the letters to the *Morning Post*, there is further evidence that the abbey and its setting regularly recurred as an image in Wordsworth's mind. It seems to have flashed upon his 'inward eye' as pleasantly as the celebrated daffodils, for in 1823 there is a parenthetic reference in a poem addressed to Lady Flemming on the foundation of Rydal Church and a few years earlier in a letter to his good friend Henry Crabb Robinson, who, having visited the ruins, had not been as impressed as Wordsworth would have liked. Wordsworth had specifically charged him to visit the ruins in a letter giving him detailed advice on what to see and do during his projected Lakes holiday. On learning of Robinson's lack of enthusiasm, Wordsworth partly apologizes and partly rebukes him: 'How came you to quarrel with Furness Abbey – your old enemy bad weather must have persecuted you into a bad humour. . . . Furness Abbey presents some grand points of view, which you must have missed – The Architecture . . . is dilapidated far beyond the point where entireness may advantageously be infringed upon. . . . But after all why not be thankful for what has been done and yet remains?' Most visitors wandering around this monument today will surely side with Wordsworth in this argument.

In August 1794 Wordsworth spent a summer holiday at Rampside, almost on the southernmost tip of Furness. (Dorothy too spent some time there, at the home of their cousin Mrs Barber.) He refers to this holiday in 'Elegiac Stanzas Suggested by a picture of Peele Castle':

> I was thy neighbour once, thou rugged Pile!
> Four summer weeks I dwelt in sight of thee:
> I saw thee every day; and all the while
> Thy form was sleeping in a glassy sea.
> So pure the sky, so quiet was the air!
> So like, so very like, was day to day!

Despite the unmemorable nature of each day there, however, he was to connect with that holiday one of those major events in international affairs which are so dramatic that for evermore in our minds the event is inextricably connected with the place where we first heard the news. For Wordsworth, one such event was the death of Robespierre, of which he heard almost casually as he crossed Ulverston Sands at low tide. He paints a vivid and timeless picture of a motley collection of foot travellers, coaches and carts and horse-riders

Wading, in loose procession through the shallow Stream
Of inland water . . .

with the sea at a safe distance. He found the scene so
pleasing to look on that in his own words he 'paused,
Unwilling to proceed'. He casually enquired of a passing
traveller 'if any news were stirring'. He would remember
the laconic reply for the rest of his life: 'Robespierre was
dead.' The news elated him, and he crossed those 'open
sands' with all the excitement and expectation of a fell-
walker springing up a favourite mountain on the first day
of his holiday. And as he crossed, memories came flooding
back of that schoolboy ride through the nearby Vale of
Nightshade and the noisy crew of boys, of which he was
part,

> . . . hastening to their distant home,
> Along the margin of the moonlight Sea,
> We beat with thundering hooves the level Sand.

The death of Robespierre has also enabled scholars to
date quite accurately to August 1794 the time when
Wordsworth holidayed at Rampside, where he was probably joined by Dorothy for a couple of weeks. They stayed
at what is now the Clarke's Arms, a seaside hotel popular
at weekends with Barrovians seeking a bracing breath of
sea air and a bar lunch.

A little south of Rampside lie Piel Island and the ruins of
Peele Castle, which Wordsworth saw daily during his
summer holiday. Over ten years later, in 1806, he saw in
London a painting of the castle by his friend and patron Sir
George Beaumont. The memory of that distant holiday
mingled with the sharper and more immediate memory of
his brother John, drowned in a shipwreck the previous
year. The sensitive Beaumont had apparently deliberate-
ly avoided drawing Wordsworth's attention to the painting, sensing that it would reawaken his grief, since the
picture showed a ship in a stormy sea. Wordsworth later
wrote to Beaumont confessing that his picture 'was to me a
very moving one', and the poem it inspired was justly

admired – 'Elegiac Stanzas suggested by a Picture of Peele Castle in a Storm'. Wordsworth contrasts the perfect calmness of the sea he had known a decade before with the 'deadly swell' depicted in the painting. With the knowledge of John's' death still fresh in his mind, and having read the horrific details of the shipwreck in an eye-witness account, he realizes that he can never again enjoy the glassy sea he viewed from Rampside, and this new knowledge is curiously calming:

> Not for a moment could I now behold
> A smiling sea, and be what I have been:
> The feeling of my loss will ne'er be old;
> This, which I know, I speak with mind serene.

Conishead Priory, three miles south-east of Ulverston, where the Leven Estuary widens out into Ulverston Sands on one side and Cartmel Sands on the other, has recently been given, as the saying goes, a new lease of life and is once again a tourist attraction where visitors are made welcome. It is often mentioned by Wordsworth and his contemporaries, and guidebook writers of the time rarely fail to recommend a visit. In his own *Guide*, Wordsworth suggested that tourists approaching the Lakes by the sands route should make a little diversion in Furness to enjoy the view from Urswick and then pass through the grounds of Conishead Priory.

Black Combe is one of those hills which Lake District lovers more often mention as having seen rather than climbed. Its somewhat detached and isolated position in the far south-west of the National Park (the boundary seems flatteringly to have been drawn so as specifically to include it) makes it prominent from many unexpected viewpoints.

Wordsworth climbed the hill and wrote categorically in a footnote to the poem he composed that, 'the summit commands a more extensive view than any other point in Britain.' Although its height on OS maps seems unimpressive by central Lakeland standards (a mere 1,970 feet), its proximity to the sea is the secret of the extensive view and also the reason why it can be seen from many distant vantage-points. Appropriately, Wordsworth met on Black Combe the eminent surveyor Colonel Mudge, a major-general in the Royal Artillery and a distinguished mathematician. He was elected a member of the Royal Society in 1798 and had won many accolades when Wordsworth saw him at work on Black Combe. But despite the honours heaped upon him, he must surely have prized as much as any of them the inscription which the poet composed for walkers to read as they ascended this 'huge eminence'. Entitled 'Written with a slate pencil on a stone, on the side of the mountain of Black Comb', it is both a tribute to Mudge and an incentive to flagging walkers to take heart from the Colonel's energy and application:

> . . . on the summit whither thou art bound,
> A geographic Labourer pitched his tent,
> With books supplied and instruments of his art,
> To measure height and distance; lonely task,
> Week after week pursued! . . .

Mudge told Wordsworth that on one occasion he had been so absorbed in his scientific studies on the summit that darkness fell so suddenly that he had not time to put away his outspread map and instruments before he was plunged into total blackness. It is understandable that this man's example so impressed Wordsworth, with its romantic notion of the man alone against the elements in the remotest of places, but who at the same time was engaged in a totally absorbing pursuit of scientific (and highly useful) knowledge.

The meeting took place by chance in 1813, when Wordsworth was forty-three and his life halfway over, at the time when he had forsaken those heady youthful ideals ('. . . bliss was it in that dawn to be alive, But to be young was very heaven,' he had said of his stay in Revolutionary France) and had just embarked on what was to be a long career as a government servant as Distributor of Stamps. Did he ever look back on that chance encounter on Black

Combe and envy the Colonel's work, which was not only skilful and laudable but also gave him

> Full many a glimpse (but sparingly bestowed
> On timid man) of Nature's processes
> Upon the exalted hills. . . .

It is interesting to compare the Mudge incident with another reference to Black Combe, included in the 'Itinerary Poems of 1835' in which there is a romantic notion of a shepherd who, in the course of his daily tasks, must often feel a sense of wonder in the face of nature's extraordinary power. The shepherd, like the Colonel, is alone:

> Ranging the heights of Scawfell or Black Comb,
> In his lone course the Shepherd oft will pause,
> And strive to fathom the mysterious laws
> By which the clouds, arrayed in light or gloom,
> On Mona settle, and the shapes assume
> Of all her peaks and ridges. . . .

In 1811 the family had decided on a seaside break and William took Mary, Thomas and Catherine to the coast near Bootle. He described it as a 'dreary place' but they stayed nearly four weeks. They had previously tried Duddon Bridge, which they found very pleasant, but they thought the water not salt enough for the children to receive the therapeutic properties of sea bathing. They also found the tides inconvenient. Their stay in Bootle gave Wordsworth a chance to renew a friendship with the Reverend Dr James Satterthwaite, the Rector of Bootle and a friend from Cambridge days. They were to see more of him in later years when he became Rector of Lowther. The cottage where they stayed was only seven minutes' walk from the coast, and they enjoyed a view of the Isle of Man from their windows – when the weather allowed. Wordsworth, who had abandoned work on his poem 'The Excursion', hoped that the 'murmuring ocean' would inspire him.

The family took the opportunity of going on long walks

in the area and visiting the surrounding sights. They were disappointed to find that the owner of Muncaster Castle had become something of a recluse, having 'shut himself up so with Plantations and chained gates and locks that whatever prospects he may command from his Fortification, can only be guessed at'. Today the castle is regularly open to the public, and the descendant of Wordsworth's misanthropic 'Hibernian Peer' is very welcoming. When the church at Bootle was enlarged and improved some thirty-five years later, Wordsworth expressed great satisfaction over the new zeal for church building and improvement.

Whitehaven in his day was a flourishing port, with a lucrative trade with Ireland and the United States. He remembered as a child seeing 'the white waves breaking against its quays and piers', and when Dorothy first saw the sea here as a child, she burst into tears of excitement. In later life Wordsworth was a frequent diner at the table here of Lord Lowther, who maintained 'Castle Whitehaven' as his West Cumberland seat. It is now the hospital.

Further north, at Workington, are more grand associations – this time with the Curwen family. After William's son John had married the heiress Isabella Curwen, the family saw much of West Cumberland. The marriage was a grand affair in the old church at Workington, with fifty guests seated at the breakfast, guns in the harbour being fired ceremoniously and ships raising their flags. William's third grandchild, also William, was born in the rectory at Workington, while Reverend John Wordsworth 'minded' the parish for the Curwen family.

Moresby is a little-noticed hamlet on the hectic A595 between Workington and Whitehaven, usually pronounced wrongly: it is not 'Moorsbee' but 'Morrizbee'. Its gaunt church, where John Wordsworth was rector from 1829 to 1833, seems to have been built out of proportion, the tall walls with a double row of four windows appearing much too high in relation to the size of the small tower. He arrived apprehensive about the description of the congregation which the Bishop of London had given to his father: '. . . a troublesome nest of sectaries . . .' requiring zeal tempered with moderation. A daunting enough task for even an experienced rector.

These anxieties were, however, small compared with the delight the Wordsworths shared at the prospect of having John back in their midst. If the living was a relatively poor one, Moresby did at least have the compensation of being in a part of Cumberland which was considered most salubrious. Perhaps it was the fact that Rydal Mount was some distance from the nearest stretch of coast that persuaded the Wordsworths of the efficacy of sea air as a restorative. Certainly the advantage of having their eldest son so satisfactorily placed meant a lot to both Mary and William, and during John's period of office most members of the family stayed with him at one time or another, often as convalescents. Some fifteen years previously they had contemplated dispatching Dorothy with the young Willy and Dora to the seaside as a pick-me-up, a project abandoned in favour of cold baths every morning as a way of toughening up the children for the approaching winter. Such ideas now came to the fore again, with renewed hopes that Dora's poor health might be improved with large doses of sea air and regular sea bathing. Accordingly in 1830 Dora spent a long holiday with her brother and became much improved as a result of the long walks and rides along the cliff tops.

It was the position of the church at Moresby which they all so much relished, and certainly, despite the nearby spoil heaps (now brilliantly landscaped), the view is inspiring. Wordsworth extolled in particular the magnificent sunsets over the sea and much enjoyed observing the plentiful bird life along the coast. On one extended visit he regularly walked at least twelve miles every day and rode a good deal as well. He writes eloquently of listening in the churchyard to the sound of the sea below – a 'base harmony' to the song of the larks above. Much of the charm of travel is experiencing landscapes and situations different from one's everyday life, and Wordsworth readily admitted that this was so for him, a 'sequestered mountaineer' unused to looking out on almost boundless prospects. It was such powerful experiences which led him to compose, on his sixty-third birthday, on Easter Sunday 1833, the following lines, entitled 'On a High Part of the Coast of Cumberland':

The Sun that seemed so mildly to retire,
Flung back from distant climes a streaming fire,
Whose blaze is now subdued to tender gleams,
Prelude of night's approach with soothing dreams.
Look round; – of all the clouds not one is moving;
'Tis the still hour of thinking, feeling, loving.
Silent, and steadfast as the vaulted sky,
The boundless plain of waters seem to lie. . . .

Not only are the natural features of these surroundings awe-inspiring, but so too are the man-made features, for here is the site of an ancient Roman fort, covering some 3½ acres of ground between the churchyard and the steeply sloping ground which goes down to the sea. A Hadrianic inscription dates the stone fort to around AD 128, and there was an extensive civil settlement to the south-east. Also of impressive antiquity is the chancel arch of the old church, still occupying its original position a few dozen yards from the present building. This arch is thought to be thirteenth century and makes a striking impression on the visitor wandering among the graves both ancient and modern.

The interior of the church is more congenial than the exterior, and one may imagine Wordsworth listening to his son's sermons with a proud, if critical, ear. After one such visit, he was moved to write to Dora, who was staying with her brother, to correct John's slightly bizarre pronunciation of certain words, and he asked his daughter to pay special attention to such words as 'unaty', and 'charaty'. Notwithstanding this mild rebuke, they were all immensely proud of their son, admiring his conscientious approach and his 'sweet and powerful' voice.

The interior of the church has been modified somewhat since the Wordsworths' time, and a number of features date only from the 1880s, such as the chancel with its lovely Venetian east window. The pine ceiling and the stained glass also belong to this later period. The church is dedicated to St Bridget, the Irish saint who was born AD 453 in the Ulster town of Dundalk.

On the other side of the lane from the church is a building which the Wordsworths must have frequently regretted was not the rectory – Moresby Hall, a truly fascinating work of architecture, built around 1700. The façade is well worth closer inspection, with its picturesque mullioned windows, decorative pediments and neatly arranged bays. The whole effect is reminiscent of some of the older Oxford colleges and comes as a great surprise set almost cheek by jowl with the nearby coal tips. (The tips were subjected to a £3 million reclamation scheme in 1983, a magnificent example to other areas so blighted.)

Although this house is the nearest habitation to the church, John was obliged to take bachelor lodgings at Mill Grove on the opposite side of the main road. He lodged in a house with an attractive garden and paid £25 per annum for his rooms and fire, with such items as candles and washing as extras to be found from his by no means over-generous income of £120 a year. But he was happy enough and was able to have members of his family to stay with him for long stretches at a time. Also his new home was very accessible, with the Ambleside coach passing by on alternate days and the mail coach daily.

After his marriage to Isabella Curwen, this accommodation proved unsuitable for such an important wife, and they took out leases on two houses in an attempt to find the most convenient home. Neither proved wholly satisfactory for Isabella's fragile health, and the couple spent a good deal of time at her parents' home, Workington Hall.

Among the important guests who stayed with them during this period was Walter Savage Landor, who arrived at Whitehaven Harbour by steamboat from Liverpool in the summer of 1832. In March of that year John and Isabella presented William with his first grandchild, a daughter who was christened Jane Stanley Wordsworth. Perhaps their belief in the beneficial effects of the Cumbrian Coast were well founded if Jane's longevity is any guide, for she lived to the ripe old age of seventy-nine, dying in 1912.

Certainly the sea air seems to have been a tonic for Wordsworth, now in his sixties. He recounts with relish one particular excursion from this time, when he rides out to Arlecdon to see George Wilkinson, the former curate of Moresby. On another occasion he takes that spectacular cliff walk along the coast to St Bees, a prominent sandstone headland which juts out into the sea and which is still famed for its beauty and wealth of bird life. He and John set out from Whitehaven on a memorable day which gave them views of the whole length of the Cumbrian coast right down to the distinctive outline of Black Combe and north to the Scottish hills, with the distant Isle of Man in full view across the sea. Wordsworth was captivated by the scene.

In 1833 he had taken a steamboat trip to the Isle of Man and had been moved to write a poem whose theme had suggested itself to him as he was sailing off St Bees Head. It contains an image which shows how he always retained a sense of wonder at the beauty of nature, especially when hard physical exertion and mental concentration were the precursors of those moments of joy:

> . . . no one plucks the rose,
> Whose proffered beauty in safe shelter blows
> 'Mid a trim garden's summer luxuries,
> With joy like his who climbs, on hands and knees,
> For some rare plant, yon Headland of St Bees.

The River Duddon has its source among the high fells around Wrynose, flowing through Dunnerdale and joining the sea just south of Broughton in Furness. It is a valley of unsurpassed beauty but, because it contains no lake, is less popular than the other central Lakeland dales. It was a valley which William and Mary greatly admired and which inspired William to write a sequence of sonnets. Beginning among the high hills, 'remote from every taint of sordid industry', he follows the river down to the sea, just had he often followed the course of the valley.

The sonnets were composed over several years, but the discovery of the love letters written during their middle years gives extra significance to the couple's walk together through the area in the summer of 1811. They had been to Bootle for a seaside family holiday, and the children returned by a different route, leaving William and Mary to savour the peace, the quiet and the beauty of the valley. They took their time and lunched in the porch of the church at Ulpha, where they 'Passed two hours there and in the beautiful churchyard'. Wordsworth admits that their pace was so slow and their stops so many that it was half past four in the afternoon before they reached the Newfield Inn, at Seathwaite. Both the inn at Seathwaite and the church at Ulpha are still there, and much of the countryside is relatively unchanged since their time, apart from the forestry plantations.

Like so many of the remoter chapels, the 'kirk' at Ulpha seems to owe more to the builders of barns than to the architects of cathedrals: homely, unpretentious and in perfect harmony with its surroundings. The lychgate and the path up to the porch seem positively to beckon you inside. No wonder the Wordsworths lingered so long, in the manner of courting couples. Sit still in the churchyard and the sound of the river makes a pleasing accompaniment to the view. Wordsworth recommends both contemplative rest here and peregrination:

> . . . there to pace, and mark the summit's hoar
> Of distant moon-lit mountains faintly shine,
> Soothed by the unseen river's gentle roar.

The church is proud of its associations with the poet, and the handsomely produced guide quotes his line, 'The Kirk of Ulpha, to the pilgrim's eye, is welcome as a star.'

Although the next church, at Seathwaite, is less than three miles to the north, it was in Wordsworth's day a whole county away, with the River Duddon marking the boundary between Cumberland and Lancashire. And though Seathwaite Chapel is a much-loved building, it is not the one Wordsworth knew and wrote about. The older chapel was replaced by the present one in 1874, much to John Ruskin's disgust – he was then living at Brantwood in the neighbouring valley of Coniston.

But it is less the church and more the life and example of the Reverend Robert Walker, parson of the old church for well over sixty years, from 1736 to 1801, which is the object of most admiration. He has become a legendary figure in the area, and in an extensive note to the Duddon Sonnets Wordsworth contributed a memoir which has consolidated his fame. It is the moving story of a man who tirelessly dedicated his life to his parishioners. His monument is no less memorable for not being marble; it consists of a lichen-spattered stone mounted with a sundial and a brass plate which explains the stone's significance as it reveals the hard-working life of a man who preached, taught and farmed:

> THIS STONE WAS USED
> AT GATESKELL FARM
> ABOUT THE MIDDLE OF THE
> 18th CENTURY AS A STOOL
> FOR CLIPPING SHEEP BY
> THE REV ROBERT WALKER
> VICAR OF THE
> PARISH OF SEATHWAITE
> REVERED BY THE TITLE OF
> WONDERFUL WALKER

There are several stepping-stones across the river, though the one which is the subject of Wordsworth's sonnet is not by any means the best known today, being a little way from the public road. For those who enjoy getting off the beaten track, it is worth the trouble of seeking it out. The walk begins just half a mile north of Ulpha Church, and south of a small conifer plantation. From the road a private drive, just wide enough for one car, goes through a metal gate to a house called High Hurst. This is the public footpath which goes across the fields and down to the stepping-stones beyond the cottage, which is midway between the road and the river. Over the

porch of the house is a rectangular stone with the initials
'E.A.' and the date '1765'. A gatepost with four holes is also
marked with the carved letters '1765 E.A.' At the river
bank there is

> . . . what might seem a zone
> Chosen for ornament – stone matched with stone
> In studied symmetry, with interspace
> For the clear waters to pursue their race. . . .

Coming across them just as Wordsworth describes makes
up for the disappointment that Seathwaite Chapel is not
the building he knew, though the sonnet on the former
chapel is hardly a description or celebration of that particular building as much as a eulogy on the Reverend
Walker:

> Whose good works formed an endless retinue:
> A Pastor such as Chaucer's verse portrays;
> Such as the heaven-taught skill of Herbert drew;
> And tender Goldsmith crowned with deathless praise!

Undercrag, the farmhouse where 'the Wonderful
Walker' lived, can still be seen just north of the chapel, and
just to the south the Newfield Inn still offers hospitality to
travellers and tourists. Here in the autumn of 1804 William and Dorothy Wordsworth stayed. They were delighted with the friendly reception they were given, and their
supper, costing one shilling, included char (a freshwater
fish prized in the Lake District) which had been caught
from the nearby tarn. Dorothy could hardly contain her
glee that the supper, overnight, breakfast, horse and ale
came to a total of 4s. 6d. They were further delighted with
the countryside, the friendly people and the snug cottages
half hidden by the rocks which are still a feature today of
'this our most romantic of all our vales'.

This devotion to the Duddon never left them. A few
weeks before his sixtieth birthday, in March 1830, Wordsworth was again out this way. On horseback, and accompanied by his eldest son, who was returning to his wife in

Whitehaven, he remarked on the picturesque cottages embowered with fir trees, sycamores and laurel. The previous May they had been enchanted by the morning lights and shadows as the delicate mist dispersed. And the 'Roman Camp' at Hardknott left an abiding impression:

> Till nightly lamentations, like the sweep
> Of winds – though winds were silent –
> Struck a deep
> And lasting terror through the ancient Hold.

The Wordsworths' excursions to the River Duddon would often include visits to the more westerly valleys – Wasdale, Ennerdale and remoter spots such as Devoke Water. Although there are few well-known poems or references to these spots, they were nonetheless greatly appreciated. One of the problems was the difficulty of access, which still makes these western beauty spots less frequented than central Lakeland. Writing to a correspondent in 1826, Wordsworth advises a journey out to Wastwater but adds, significantly, that it is for tourists who have time and strength to spare. When he and Dorothy visited Wasdale in 1804, they were entertained and accompanied by a 'statesman farmer' as there was no inn at the head of the valley.

In the summer of 1832 he took Walter Savage Landor from Wasdale over into Borrowdale and hence to Greta Hall to see Southey. Landor had been staying at Croockhead in Nether Wasdale, described by Wordsworth as a very pretty residence among the sublimities of Wasdale. A better choice could hardly have been hit upon for Landor, who had written:

> I know not whether I am proud,
> But this I know, I hate the crowd.

The crowd is still less apparent here than in many other Lakeland valleys.

Ennerdale too is protected by its remoteness from the worst ravages of mass tourism. When Wordsworth and

Coleridge were on their celebrated walking tour in 1799, they heard in Ennerdale the woeful tale of Jerome Bowman, a shepherd who had died when he broke a leg on the fells. Then Bowman's son fell to his death from a crag whilst walking in his sleep. Wordsworth incorporated much of the story into his pastoral poem 'The Brothers' which vividly describes the unmistakable Pillar Rock which hangs over Ennerdale, where the young shepherd came to grief after dozing off in the sunshine. The priest tells the story to the surviving brother, returned to the valley after a long absence at sea, and unrecognized by the clergyman. Thus the brother learns of the tragedy which took place on Pillar's 'aery summit crowned with heath'.

'The Brothers' is also of interest as being one of the first poems to be composed after William and Dorothy settled at Dove Cottage a couple of months after the walking tour with Coleridge. The opening of the poem, which is composed around an imaginary conversation between the surviving brother and the parson of Ennerdale, shows that in some people's minds tourists were already becoming a nuisance as early as 1799:

> These Tourists, heaven preserve us! needs must live
> A profitable life: some glance along,
> Rapid and gay, as if the earth were air,
> And they were butterflies to wheel about
> Long as their summer lasted: some, as wise,
> Perched on the forehead of a jutting crag,
> Pencil in hand and book upon the knee,
> Will look and scribble, scribble on and look,
> Until a man might travel twelve stout miles,
> Or reap an acre of his neighbour's corn.

9

Youth's Golden Gleam

Penrith and the Lowther Estates

Pooley Bridge at the north end of Ullswater is a good place to embark on a tour of many fascinating places associated with the Wordsworths which are often almost unknown. On the 'town' side of the bridge which gives its name to the village, there is a footpath which goes towards the lake – although a private drive, it is a public right of way on foot. The start is marked by a rather impressive pair of gateposts, almost six feet high surmounted by two perfectly carved stone spheres. Now gateless, but recalling a more leisurely age, this drive soon subdivides into two separate footpaths. The right-hand one goes towards the lake, with glimpses, and later full views, of Eusemere, a house which all the Wordsworths visited over a long span of time.

Eusemere, in the early years of the nineteenth century, was the home of Thomas Clarkson, a man who devoted his life to the abolition of the slave trade, and with whom, in 1802, Dorothy, Mary and William stayed. Fifteen years later it was to become the home of a member of the Wordsworth family – but more of that anon. In 1802 Dorothy was as usual an enthusiastic admirer of a friend's house: '. . . most enchanting . . . the prospect from the house one of the finest among the Lakes'; and on a return visit over twenty years later she still found it 'very pretty', though by this time many of Clarkson's plantings had grown up and she felt obliged to add to her description: 'nothing wanting but the ax', a judgement still apt, though

further on there are better views of the house until, across
the fields, there comes into sight a building of regular
plan, a door in the middle of the front with two rows of four
windows on either side. There are good views too of the fine
three-arched bridge which spans the River Eamont to the
right. Soon the river bank gives way to the lake shore, and
the visitor, unless a patron of Park Foot caravan site (and
so allowed to cross the fields towards the road), is obliged
to either continue along the shore by Gale Bay and Water-
side House or to retrace his steps and rejoin the portion of
Eusemere's lane which is a right of way, and where a short
path goes south-east to join the Sharrow Bay–Howtown
road at the 511-feet contour. From this path there is a view
of Eusemere's east wing, across a bank which in the spring
is a mass of daffodils. At the public road, a left turn follows
the tarmac back into Pooley Bridge. Dunmallet shows its
most impressive face from the lane at the cattle-grid, the
nearest point at which the public right of way approaches
to Eusemere.

The Wordsworths' associations with Eusemere spanned
many years, and even after the Clarksons returned to
their native East Anglia, William and Dorothy kept up a
regular correspondence with them all their lives, and met
them from time to time in London. From Wordsworth's
first visit to their Ullswater estate in 1799 during his
walking tour with Coleridge, it was clear they would
become good friends. There is a flattering account of him
written by Mrs Clarkson after their first meeting at Eusemere, when he and Coleridge spent a full day in their
company: '. . . a fine commanding figure . . . rather handsome & looks as if he was born to be a great prince or a
great general. He seems very fond of C. laughing at all his
jokes & taking all opportunities of showing him off & to
crown all he has the manners of a gentleman.'

Soon after this was written, William and Dorothy took
Dove Cottage, and their proximity to Ullswater enabled
their friendship to flourish. By January 1802 they were
staying a full month with the Clarksons, and in the spring
of that same year they stayed with them again. After a
difficult journey returning from Durham, Wordsworth

found the Clarkson hospitality particularly welcome: he arrived well into the evening, '. . . more tired than I should otherwise have been, on account of not being able to ride fast for the horses shoes. . . .' Dorothy was already at Eusemere, eagerly awaiting her brother's return, though when he arrived, she had gone for an evening stroll along the lakeshore towards Martindale. A maid was despatched to tell her of William's return: 'I believe I screamed, when she said so, and ran on. . . .' It was clearly a hospitable house, and Mary was likewise drawn into the Clarkson circle and spent time at Eusemere.

'If walls could speak . . .' the saying goes. And if these walls of Eusemere could speak, they would tell a tale not just of friendly hospitality but also of one of those men who command admiration. For in this house Clarkson did much of his preparatory work for the abolition of the slave trade. Although Wilberforce's name springs first to mind in relation to this great cause of the nineteenth century, there is no doubt that Thomas Clarkson played a key role in the success of the legislation. When the abolitionists triumphed in 1807, Wordsworth wrote a sonnet 'To Thomas Clarkson, on the Final Passing of the Bill for the Abolition of the Slave Trade'. His visits to Eusemere had left him in no doubt as to Clarkson's total commitment to the cause: Clarkson was a 'true yoke-fellow of Time' to borrow his own resounding phrase:

> CLARKSON! It was an obstinate hill to climb: . . .
> The bloodstained-writing is for ever torn;
> And thou henceforth wilt have a good man's calm,
> A great man's happiness; thy zeal shall find
> Repose at length, firm friend of human kind!

After the Clarksons vacated Eusemere and sold the property to Lord Lowther in 1804, the Wordsworths continued to visit the house as guests of the new tenants, the Miss Greens. The connection with Eusemere was also maintained when Mary's brother, Tom Hutchinson, took the nearby farm at Park House and when William's cousin Captain John Wordsworth remarried and made it his home until his death in September 1819. (It was this cousin who in 1800 handed over the command of the East Indiaman *Earl of Abergavenny* to William's brother John.) When the Captain settled in with his new bride, Dorothy spent two days at Eusemere and wrote to Mrs Clarkson of the warm welcome she received, of the captain's 'judicious choice' and of the relatively few changes which had been made since the Clarksons moved all those years ago. She was especially delighted that the lodging-rooms had exactly the same wallpaper, still as fresh and clean as it had appeared to her in 1803, looking '. . . as if they had been put up this summer'.

Barton Church is two miles north of Pooley Bridge, just to the west of the B5320 road, and is approached by a clearly signposted lane. It is a low, sturdy church with a squat, picturesque tower set in open countryside surrounded on all sides by farmed land. Although placed in a fairly remote position, the churchyard is clearly well cared for, and there is a decidedly welcoming air to the building. For once, here is a church proud of its Wordsworth associations, and the printed guide has a section headed 'The Wordsworths and Barton'. So many other guides to the 'Wordsworth' churches either ignore the connection or simply give it a cursory mention.

In the chancel the body of William's grandfather, Richard Wordsworth, was laid to rest. He was born in 1690 in Yorkshire and was the first member of the family to come to Westmorland, beginning a long and honourable connection with the region which continues to the present day. He held some distinguished offices in the locality, being at times Clerk of the Peace, Agent to the Lowther Estates and Receiver General of the County. The inscription marking the grave reads: 'Here lieth interred Mr Richard Wordsworth of Sockbridge June 25th 1760 aged 70 years.' His wife's inscription is hidden, but there is another concerning Ann Myers, William's aunt, the daughter of Richard: 'Sacred to the memory of Ann Myers wife to the Reverend Thomas Myers Curate of this Parish and Rector of Croglin in the County of Cumberland.' She married in 1763 and died in 1787, when her son John and

William were both undergraduates at St John's College, Cambridge. Two more tablets are to the memory of Captain Wordsworth's wives, Anne and Elisabeth.

Nearby is the Myers' former house, a farm tucked away on a steep and narrow short lane which links the B5320 with the higher road which goes to Celleron and Askham.

A short distance along the road to Celleron, then left, there is soon a junction with the B5320 which goes into Sockbridge, where William's father owned an estate, inherited by Richard, his eldest brother, who lived at Sockbridge House, now renamed Wordsworth House, an elegant building close to the older centre of the village. Before Richard left to work as a lawyer in London, and during his occasional returns home, there are references to visits to his house here. Around Christmas 1815, for instance, first William and Dorothy, and later William and Mary visited Sockbridge. After Richard's death the estate was held in trust for his son John, known as 'Sockbridge John' to distinguish him from other John Wordsworths in the extended family.

Another mile further along the road towards Penrith is the village of Yanwath, where another friend of the Wordsworths, the Quaker Thomas Wilkinson, made his home at 'The Grotto', now a private residence but easily seen from the right of way which goes close to the house. Again this is a friendship which dates from the return of Dorothy and William to the Lake District, and one which lasted until the death of Wilkinson in 1836. During their stays at Eusemere they saw much of their friend, who after their first meeting wrote, 'I had lately a young poet seeing me that sprung originally from the next village,' referring to Sockbridge, the patrimony of William's father.

Wilkinson's passionate interest in gardening and landscaping impressed Wordsworth, who at times was positively obsessed with them – the subject once tempting him to write the longest letter of his life, later published as an appendix to the *Guide* under the heading 'Of Building and Gardening and Laying Out of Grounds'. In this letter (to Sir George Beaumont) he refers to the work Wilkinson had done on his Eamont estate: '. . . in twining pathways along the banks of the river, making little cells and bowers with inscriptions of his own writing, all very pretty'.

To reach the house, the visitor must turn left off the road from Sockbridge to Eamont Bridge, where a few yards along the track by the railway bridge there is a clear sign directing through a gate and onto the right of way, which, although it avoids the private immediate gardens of 'The Grotto', nevertheless affords excellent views of the house and leads to a high bank overlooking the Eamont which is wooded on the steep slopes. It was here that Wilkinson laid out the winding walks which took Wordsworth's fancy and which must also have drawn the admiration of Lord Lowther, who appointed Wilkinson *'Arbiter Elegantiarum'*, or 'Master of the Grounds', for his nearby estates at Lowther.

Continuing along the B5320, crossing the motorway and then turning right for a few hundred yards along the A6, on the left is the B6262 which leads to the high walls marked on the map as Brougham Hall, rented by Wordsworth's cousin Captain John Wordsworth after his retirement from the sea. William and Mary stayed here in 1805 with their relative. In 1810 Brougham Hall was inherited by Wordsworth's arch political enemy Henry (later Lord) Brougham. Close by the walls, and once linked by a bridge across the road, is another historic gem – Brougham (pronounced 'broom') Chapel. Half a mile to the north-east is Brougham Castle, commanding the confluence of the Rivers Eamont and Lowther, best seen from the top of the vertiginous south-west tower. In Book VI of 'The Prelude', Wordsworth describes the setting:

> . . . The gentle banks
> Of Eamont, hitherto unnam'd in song,
> and that monastic Castle, on a Flat
> Low-standing by the margin of the stream. . . .

The castle is now well cared for by the Department of the Environment, which prudently dissuades children from climbing the battlements. William and Dorothy, as chil-

dren from Penrith, experienced a *'frisson de terreur'*
here:

> My sister and myself, when having climbed
> In danger through some window's open space,
> We looked abroad, or on the Turret's head
> Lay listening to the wild flowers and the grass,
> As they gave out their whispers to the wind. . . .

This fine passage from the early version of 'The Prelude'
becomes curiously muted in the final version:

> Catching from tufts of grass and hare-bell flowers
> Their faintest whisper from the passing breeze,
> Given out while mid-day heat oppressed the plains. . . .

From the battlements it is obvious why this site has
been chosen for strategic reasons from Roman times,
being not only at the confluence of two rivers but also the
focus for roads north to Carlisle, south to Chester, south-
east across the Pennines and south-west towards the
Lakeland hills. In his ballad-style poem 'Song at the Feast
of Brougham Castle', Wordsworth tells of the happy day of
celebration when Lord Henry Clifford was restored to his
rightful place in the castle after being reared among the
north Lakeland hills, living the life of a shepherd. There,
true to the ancient tradition of such stories, he became
inseparable from the landscape around him:

> To his side the fallow-deer
> Came, and rested without fear;
> The eagle, lord of land and sea,
> Stooped down to pay him fealty. . . .

And so, formed by the rustic life around him, when he was
restored to the castle he and his subjects predictably lived
happily ever after. In the local folk memory of the area he
is known long after his death as 'the good Lord Clifford',
and his warlike antecedents are represented by the unused armour and weapons in the great hall to which
he now returns, moulded by his gentle upbringing and

further example to Wordsworth of the child being father of the man:

> His daily teachers had been woods and rills,
> The silence that is in the starry sky
> The sleep that is among the lonely hills.

Just two miles out of Penrith, on the A66 road to Appleby, is 'the Countess' Pillar'. It is easily missed on this fast stretch of road as the route straightens to follow the course of a Roman road. The best way to find it is to look out for two rather unromantic landmarks as you leave Penrith behind; the first is the line of pylons under which the road passes, and almost immediately on the left is the second landmark: the entrance to the sewage works. On the opposite side of the road on a raised bank are the twenty-foot-high pillar and adjoining stone table, surrounded by protective iron railings. The pillar is the subject of a sonnet by Wordsworth and is handsomely decorated with heraldic devices and an inscription which records that it was erected in 1656 by the much-loved Lady Anne Clifford, Countess Dowager of Pembroke (a one-time occupant of Brougham Castle), as a memorial to her final parting with her mother, the Countess of Cumberland, on 2nd April 1616. Typically of the charitable Lady Anne, she was not content that the memory of her mother should be confined solely to an impressive pillar: hence the stone table close by, on which was distributed an annuity of £4 per annum to the poor of the parish of Brougham on the anniversary day of the parting.

> .... Many a stranger passing by
> Has with that Parting mixed a filial sigh,
> Blest its humane Memorial's fond endeavour;
> And, fastening on those lines an eye tear-glazed,
> Has ended, though no clerk, with 'God be praised'.

The final line echoes the phrase '*Laus Deo*' on the pillar itself.

Wordsworth penned this sonnet in the autumn of 1831

on his return from a tour of Scotland. The area around Penrith held a rich store of memories for him and Dorothy, for they had spent time there in their early days, and his wife Mary knew the area even more intimately. He had always been impressed by the many historical associations of the area with its abounding evidence of prehistoric settlement, Roman occupation and medieval life. The stories and legends which these associations held were a vein which he often quarried for subjects for poetry.

On this same Penrith–Appleby road was the so-called Hart's-horn Tree, now gone, which is unsurprising since the story associated with it goes back well over six hundred years to 1333. In that year Edward Baliol, King of Scotland, came to stay with the first Robert de Clifford, one of whose castles is close by at Brougham. The two noblemen ran a stag a considerable distance with 'a single greyhound', finishing at this spot where the tree grew. Both stag and hound were completely exhausted. The stag leapt over a fence and died immediately. The greyhound attempted to leap the fence but failed, and also expired. In memory of the event the stag's antlers were nailed to a nearby tree and a rhyme was appended giving equal honour to the stag and the dog, whose name was Hercules:

> Hercules kill'd Hart a greese,
> And Hart a greese killed Hercules.

In a note to the poem Wordsworth explained how the tree impressed him even in its 'decayed state'. Apparently the horns were so overgrown by the tree that a further pair were nailed to the trunk, and the story was clearly kept alive by constant retelling to the many travellers who passed this way in the days when the route was much more important than it is now.

> Here stood an oak, that long had borne affixed
> To his huge trunk, or with more subtle art,
> Among its withering topmost branches mixed,
> The Palmy antlers of a hunted Hart,
> Whom the dog Hercules pursued. . . .

But if the oak is gone, there are still many other historic remnants in this locality, most of which the Wordsworths knew well.

Penrith is proud of its associations with the Wordsworths, and even the most unobservant visitor to the town cannot fail to notice the plaques which have been erected on various buildings. A rectangular plaque on the drapery shop in Devonshire Street records that 'William and Dorothy Cookson grandparents of William and Dorothy Wordsworth lived here'. William Cookson was a Penrith mercer and linen draper who married Dorothy Crackanthorpe of Newbiggin Hall. He died in 1787 and is buried in the churchyard. The parish registers record the marriage of their daughter Ann to John Wordsworth, whose own father had also died in Penrith, in 1760. Thus speak the registers: 'John Wordsworth of the Parish of Cockermouth, bachelor, and Ann Cookson, of this Parish, spinster, and minor: married in this Church by Licence this Fifth day of February, 1766, by me, John Cowper, vicar, in the presence of Eliz. Threlkeld and J. W. H. Cowper.' Dorothy's name also appears in the registers as a witness to the marriage in October 1788 of her uncle the Reverend William Cookson to Dorothy Cowper.

The church itself is dedicated to St Andrew and, although close to the busy main thoroughfare of this bustling market town, still retains an air of peace and calm. It is a pleasing combination of classical Georgian architecture and some much earlier features, notably the Norman tower with its immensely thick walls and castellated turret. The nave was rebuilt after a fire and was completed in 1722. The main features of the church as seen today were thus the ones known to the Wordsworths. Inside, the three-sided gallery is unusual, and the brass candelabra suspended from the ceiling must surely have attracted the attention of William and Dorothy as their eyes wandered around during their early services. Both candelabra were designed to hold twenty-four candles and were given to the people of Penrith to mark their loyalty during the Jacobite Rising of 1745.

The churchyard in which the building stands is surrounded by picturesque and ancient houses, including the sixteenth-century building which formerly housed the pupils of the Queen Elizabeth Grammar School. The school which William and Dorothy are thought to have attended is the quaint red-sandstone building which now forms part of the Tudor Restaurant. This gabled edifice with its mullioned windows was probably Dame Birkett's school, and here William, Dorothy and Mary Hutchinson shared their young lives, just as they were to share their adult lives at Rydal and Grasmere. Here they learned by heart passages from the Bible and from the *Spectator* essays. 'The Dame', wrote William, 'did not affect to make theologians or logicians but she taught to read and she practised the memory . . . notably by rote. . . .' Dame Birkett died in 1790 at the age of eighty-five, and today thousands of schoolchildren study not the *Spectator* essays of her school lessons but more likely passages from the work of her famous pupil.

In Portland Place stands the former town hall, now housing the public library. A plaque on the side of the building reads: 'Wordsworth House Residence of the Poet's cousin Captain John Wordsworth.' Another plaque, on the Robin Hood's Inn, records that Wordsworth's friend and benefactor Raisley Calvert lodged here with him.

It would be surprising if more than one visitor in a thousand who visits Grasmere for its Wordsworth associations ever finds his way to the Lowther Estates for similar reasons. Today's tourists go to this fascinating corner of Lakeland largely to see either the Wildlife Park or the increasingly famous horse-trials, often attended by the Duke of Edinburgh, and yet the associations with the famous poet and his family are rich, intimate and of crucial importance in presenting an accurate and balanced portrait of Wordsworth's country.

Where better to begin this section of the journey than at Pooley Bridge at the northern tip of Ullswater, taking the B5320 towards Penrith for exactly one mile before turning right, eschewing this pleasant highway for a more exciting excursion along a narrow country lane signposted

'Celleron'. (A mile further along the main road is Barton Church, where William's grandparents, Richard and Mary, lie buried.) The lane hugs the butt end of one of the most spectacular walks in Britain – the ridge of High Street. As it curves sharply to the right, it commands, on the left, extensive views across the plain of the River Eamont towards Penrith. At first the road drops gently into Askham, but then with sudden steepness it leaves this village behind to plummet down towards the banks of the River Lowther, flowing through a precipitous and wooded gorge.

It was the trees which made the area such a favourite with the Wordsworths – the woods of Lowther had long been a haunt for the family, going right back to their Penrith childhood. 'Far-spreading' is the description Wordsworth reserved for them, and in his *Guide* he notes the varied beauty which can only be enjoyed by the pedestrian who follows the course of the river from here to Brougham, experiencing '. . . almost at every step some new feature of river, woodland, and rocky landscape'.

On the right of the road is the Church of St Peter, Askham, striking in the lightness and airiness of the building, despite its situation deep in a wooded dell. But impressive and ancient as this building is, it is only an appetite-whetter for another church barely one third of a mile distant, where Wordsworth worshipped during his stays at Lowther Castle. Surely there can be no two churches so close to each other, and each with a long and distinguished past, which present such a contrast from the point of view of their different sites. St Peter's, Askham, is hidden deep in the valley, whereas St Michael's, Lowther, commands attention from afar.

St Michael's Church and the nearby mausoleum, with the imposing ruined shell of Lowther Castle half a mile to the south, leave no doubt concerning the importance and wealth of the Lowthers who for four generations provided the main incomes for several members of Wordsworth's own family. His father, John, his uncle Richard, his sons John and Willy, as well as he himself, all depended directly or indirectly on the Lowthers, who enjoyed vast powers of appointment and preferment.

Wordsworth dedicated 'The Excursion' to his patron and friend Sir William Lowther, the first Earl of Lonsdale:

> Oft, through thy fair domains, illustrious Peer!
> In youth I roamed, on youthful pleasures bent;
> And mused in rocky cell or sylvan tent,
> Beside swift-flowing Lowther's current clear.
> – Now by thy care befriended, I appear
> Before thee, LONSDALE, and this Work present,
> A token (may it prove a monument)
> Of high respect and gratitude sincere.
> Gladly would I have waited till my task
> Had reached its close: but Life is insecure,
> And Hope full oft fallacious as a dream:
> Therefore, for what is here produced, I ask
> Thy favour; trusting that thou wilt not deem
> The offering, though imperfect, premature.

He wrote this in 1814, when he had good reason to be full of 'gratitude sincere', as the Earl had appointed him Distributor of Stamps the previous year.

The Lowther Estates are still 'fair domains', and the river below is still 'swift-flowing' with clear currents. The façade of Lowther Castle, with its turrets and towers, looks as a fairy-tale château should look. The castle, built between 1806 and 1811, was unfortunately too extravagant for present-day use and was largely demolished in 1957, leaving only part of the outer shell. There is no public access to the ruins, which in any case would, on closer inspection, lose the charm and romance they enjoy from being seen from afar. However, the records provided by earlier photographs and paintings prove that the interior of the castle amply fulfilled the expectations raised by its striking external appearance. The grand staircase, for instance, even in the photographs, shows something of the magnificence of the architecture, with soaring fluted columns and high Norman arches reminiscent of some famous cathedral. How Wordsworth, dining here with some of the most famous men of his time, must have looked back somewhat wryly to those Dove Cottage days of 'high thinking and plain living'. Nowadays one can share his feelings on one occasion when he stayed there when the Lowthers were away: '. . . what a melancholy place is a great House when the family are absent. . . .'

Wordsworth's sonnet written in 1833 against a background of increasing social unrest, and in the wake of the Reform Act of the previous year, recalls Lowther Castle in its heyday:

> LOWTHER! in thy majestic Pile are seen
> Cathedral pomp and grace, in apt accord
> With the baronial castle's sterner mien;
> Union significant of God adored,
> And charters won and guarded by the sword
> Of ancient honour; whence that goodly state
> Of polity which wise men venerate,
> And will maintain, if God his help afford.
> Hourly the democratic torrent swells;
> For airy promises and hopes suborned
> The strength of backward-looking thoughts is scorned.
> Fall if ye must, ye Towers and Pinnacles,
> With what ye symbolise; authentic Story
> Will say, Ye disappeared with England's Glory!

It is fashionable to deride these later sonnets but this one, read, as it were, 'on location' in the shadow of the castle, might dispel such prejudices.

One feature of the countryside in this area which cannot be ignored – either by the roving eye from the heights or by those in search of Wordsworth's associations – is the Border Beacon, to which he fondly referred in 'The Prelude':

> O'er paths and fields
> In all that neighbourhood, through narrow lanes
> Of eglantine, and through the shady woods,
> And o'er the Border Beacon, and the Waste
> Of naked Pools, and common Crags that lay
> Expos'd on the bare Fell, was scatter'd love,
> A spirit of pleasure and youth's golden gleam.

The Border Beacon is still a popular haunt for the children of Penrith and the town's most noticeable natural feature. Although it does not quite attain the height of one thousand feet, it is still an impressive landmark and can be scaled by an easy footpath. The views from the summit are noteworthy. In all directions there is something of interest, especially on a clear day when the Scottish hills complete a panorama which includes the Eden Valley, the Pennines, the Solway Firth, Ullswater, Saddleback and High Street. Walter Scott records seeing the Beacon alight in 1804 during the Napoleonic Wars, and in 1745 the fires blazed during the Jacobite Rising.

But it was not these great moments of history which invested the Beacon with a fascination for the boy William but a much more personal experience which took place, according to his own account, when he was five years old and which he described in 'The Prelude' as one of the first 'spots of time' which he could remember. These 'spots of time' were for Wordsworth moments of intense experience which in later years he recalled vividly and from which he constantly drew spiritual nourishment and refreshment.

The Beacon incident began when he was out riding with 'honest James . . . my encourager and guide'. By some mischance they were separated from each other, and William dismounted from his horse and stumbled upon the spot where a murderer had been hanged. Although there was little trace of the culprit's death, his initials had been carved in the turf, and each year local people cleared the grass away so that the letters 'to this hour . . . are all fresh and visible'. Suddenly coming across these letters he must have been understandably struck with terror, and he hurried back up the hill. Between a pool and the Beacon summit, he saw the figure of a girl with a pitcher on her head, struggling to walk against the strong wind. In later years he had many happy moments in this area playing with Dorothy and Mary, but he never forgot

> . . . the visionary dreariness
> Which, while I look'd all round for my lost guide,
> Did at that time invest the naked Pool,

The Beacon on the lonely Eminence,
The Woman, and her garments vex'd and toss'd
By the strong wind.

Gordon Wordsworth identified the scene of the murder
as Cowdrake Quarry, on the Eden Hall side of the Beacon,
where in 1766 Thomas Parker, a butcher, was killed by
one Thomas Nicholson. The murderer was executed at
Carlisle the following year, and his body was hung in
chains close to the scene of his crime. Apparently William
was in error about the initials, which were in fact 'TPM',
standing for 'Thomas Parker Murdered'. He had thought
that they referred to the murderer, not to the victim,
though whoever had told him the story may have been
responsible for the mistake. But the details are less important than the effect the tale had on the impressionable
child whose vivid imagination recreated the episode
immediately he was confronted by those stark initials.

10

Beauty and Grandeur

From Kirkstone Pass along the length of Ullswater

When the Wordsworths visited Ullswater from Grasmere or Rydal, they usually went over the notorious Kirkstone Pass. It is still known to Ambleside folk as 'the struggle', even though most people struggle over in the comfort of cars. When the Wordsworth children were young, William, Dorothy and Mary were sometimes obliged to carry them much of the way. For them it really was a struggle. Yet they rather admired the road in all its moods and seemed almost to delight in recounting their difficult ascents over the years. Wordsworth almost brags about the awful weather they had to endure and once seemed to have been almost proud of the violence of the storms on the summit: '. . . over Kirkstone in a fierce storm, which astonished my companions who were both Londoners'. He mentions it with awe in the *Guide* and includes a verse which regular users of the Pass will recognize as catching the distinctive atmosphere of this ancient route:

> Within the mind strong fancies work,
> A deep delight the bosom thrills,
> Oft as I pass along the fork
> Of these fraternal hills . . .
> Most potent when mists veil the sky,
> Mists that distort and magnify,
> While the coarse rushes, to the sweeping breeze,
> Sigh forth their ancient melodies!

On the descent from Ambleside, the stone which gives the Pass its name is on the left-hand side and is indeed shaped like a 'kirk' or church. De Quincey estimated that the descent into Patterdale was often made at the rate of eighteen miles an hour in the horse-drawn carriages. He describes this descent as a 'real luxury for those who enjoy the velocity of motion'.

The small lake of Brotherswater on the Ullswater side of the pass is where William and Dorothy once rested by a bridge and celebrated the arrival of fine weather after a rainstorm:

> The Cock is crowing,
> The stream is flowing,
> The small birds twitter,
> The lake doth glitter . . .
> There's joy in the mountains;
> There's life in the fountains;
> Small clouds are sailing,
> Blue sky prevailing;
> The rain is over and gone!

They usually had home-baked pies to fortify them while crossing the Pass, but on one long-remembered occasion they stayed at the inn at Patterdale where they were very well received and supplied with ham, veal cutlets, preserved plums, ale, rum, dry beds and a 'decent' breakfast.

The Wordsworths were always fond of Ullswater, and in later editions of the *Guide* William incorporated, with various modifications, extracts from Dorothy's journal for November 1805, when they were again in the area. Ten months further on in the year, they had ample opportunities to compare the contrasting effects of winter and autumn. They were now staying with their old and close friends Captain and Mrs Luff at their house at Side Farm on the east side of Goldrill Beck under the slopes of Place Fell. The best way to explore this area is not to make directly for Side Farm but to take the lake steamer from Glenridding across to Howtown and walk back along the lakeshore. There is simply no other short walk in the whole of Lakeland which can compete with this for beauty,

variety, peacefulness and ease. After walking around the
flanks of Hallin Fell with its stunning views across the
lake, there is the bay which the Wordsworths used as their
landing – Sandwick.

As he rowed along the lake, Wordsworth's curiosity was
aroused by the sight of three fisherman in the bay under
Place Fell. The scene he describes is almost identical with
a print of fishermen on Ullswater using large nets to trawl
in their catch: 'a picturesque group beneath the high and
bare crags . . . clouds and sunny gleams on the mountains'.
On landing at Sandwick they walked into Martindale,
still one of the few places where the indigenous wild red
deer can be found. They came across a shooting-lodge built
by Mr Hasell of Dalemain for use during the annual deer
chase. The room was decorated with the trophies of successful hunts, and by each set of spreading antlers was
recorded the length of the race which led to that stag's
death. Here, as so often in the remoter areas, they were
generously entertained by a 'good woman [who] treated us
with oaten cake, new and crisp'. They seemed to have
walked through Boardale and on to the Hause, which is
still marked on large scale maps as 'Chapel in the Hause',
where apparently the inhabitants of Martindale and Patterdale assembled for worship. Today it appears like many
another ruined sheepfold, though it is said that there are
still carved stones to be seen roundabout. The way continues along the shore south of Sandwick. There is no
greater modern authority on the fells of Lakeland than the
author/artist Alfred Wainwright, and he asserts that the
path between Scalehow Beck and Patterdale '. . . is the
most beautiful and rewarding walk in Lakeland'.

The Wordsworths particularly admired the view from
Blowick which they came to know well during their stays
with the Luffs at Side Farm. Even during their lifetime
the semi-wild goats which they saw on their first visit
bounding about the rocks here had gone. But the views are
still superb and we can still share many of their experiences: 'storm-stiffened' yew trees and '. . . the lemon-
coloured leaves of the birches, as the breeze turned them to
the sun, sparkle, or rather *flash*, like diamonds, and the

leafless purple twigs were tipped with globes of shining crystal.' They were so transported by the scene that they even thought of building a house on this side of Ullswater, choosing a spot and revisiting it to satisfy themselves as to its perfection. Had they fulfilled this ambition, their cottage might well have rivalled the popularity of Dove Cottage as a magnet for Wordsworthians, and how the coach-drivers would have regretted that decision as they attempted to negotiate the narrow and twisting lanes on that side of the lake!

It was while staying with the Luffs in 1805 that the Wordsworths heard, at breakfast, of the victory at Trafalgar and of the death of Lord Nelson. Dorothy burst into tears in one of the spontaneous outbursts of emotion which had always been part of her sensitive personality from childhood onwards. But the tumult of these historic events only enhanced the sense of peace they felt at the Luffs' house, where they could look out onto a serene view '. . . over the level bed of the valley . . . as level as a bowling green'.

The following year (1806) they called again on the Luffs on their way to Park House, where they were taking the children in order to avoid the outbreak of whooping cough in Grasmere. On arriving at Side Farm, baby Dora called out for 'sugar butter', presumably the Cumberland rum butter which was served traditionally at christenings but which today is mostly reserved to spoon into hot mincepies at Christmas. Little Dora had cheered their spirits as they struggled over Grisedale Hause, with her chirpy repetitions of nursery rhymes such as 'Baa Baa Black Sheep' and 'Cushy cow bonny let down thy milk'. From the Luffs' they took a boat to the landing under Soulby Fell and continued their way to Park House by foot.

Although a path by Side Farm will lead over the beck and back to Patterdale, a short way on is another property closely connected with the Wordsworths. This is the Broad How Estate, a few hundred yards to the south, where a picturesque whitewashed cottage is named 'Wordsworth's Cottage' in memory of these associations. A cluster of houses have now gathered around this site, and every one

would deservedly call forth the estate agents' most ful-
some adjectives. Wordsworth acquired the land in 1806,
but he never in fact built on it, and he sold it in 1834 to an
inn-keeper at Patterdale. What a pity that the acquisition
of such a fine property should have given him so little
satisfaction. The story goes back to the spring of 1806
when he asked his friend Thomas Wilkinson, then living
at Yanwath, to offer the sum of £800 for the farm estate.
Unknown to Wilkinson, he felt, on a point of honour and
based on a conviction that the land was worth no more
than that sum, that it would be wrong to offer the vendor a
penny more than £800. When Wilkinson was told that the
estate could change hands for £1,000, he mentioned the
fact to Lord Lowther (soon to be created Earl of Lonsdale),
who immediately insisted that Wilkinson should complete the purchase and allow him (Lord Lowther) to settle
the bill. Wilkinson, not unnaturally, agreed to this generous offer and bought the land on Wordsworth's behalf
but with Lord Lowther's money. Wordsworth was furious.
He hated getting the worst of a bargain, and though he
could not seem ungrateful by refusing Lowther's generous
gift, his sense of fair play was deeply offended: 'Strange it
is that W[ilkinson] could not perceive, that if I was unwilling to pay an exorbitant price out of my own money, I
should be still more unwilling to pay it out of another's,
especially of a person who had shown to me so much
kindness. . . .' Wordsworth was obliged to swallow his
pride and accept the situation, but his intention of building a house there and moving from Dove Cottage was
abandoned, and he let out the land for grazing.

From Broad How Goldrill Bridge crosses the beck, and
the main road leads to Glenridding. On the left, opposite
the point where the lake comes close to the road, is St
Patrick's Well, once thought to have healing properties
and a reminder of the tradition that the saint passed this
way. The origin of the name 'Patterdale' is a corruption of
'St Patrick's Dale'. The Wordsworths passed this way in
both directions and in all seasons many, many times;
several pages of the *Guide* are devoted to the lake, and
many poems were inspired by the beauty of the surround-

ing countryside. Even in the winter there were compensations: '. . . the lake was calm as a mirror, the rising sun tinged with pink Light the snow-topped mountains . . . more beautiful even than in summer . . .' wrote Dorothy in December 1815.

Dorothy especially liked Ullswater because it had not been spoilt by tourists and 'fancy builders', and in 1805 she looked on the area as a pleasing contrast to the increasing inundation of other parts of Lakeland by hordes of visitors. Of course such things are relative, and by modern standards it might seem that she exaggerated. Her attitude to Patterdale Hall at this time is a case in point, since she thought the building unsuited to the valley. She so much objected to the colour that it was changed the next summer. The Hall had been built by John Mounsey in 1796 on the site of his father's 'palace of Patterdale'. The head of the Mounsey family was always known as the King of Patterdale, a local hereditary title which originated in an ancestor's having led a party to defeat some Border raiders at Stybarrow Crag.

Today Patterdale Hall would be unlikely to raise many objections to either its design or its colour. It is an angular house which shows obvious signs of having been much extended. The terraced gardens were clearly once a great feature of the estate but today are inevitably neglected, though tidy. There are remains of a kind of knot garden on a mound, and there are still plenty of decorated stones about, which presumably once graced the balustrade and terrace walls. The long drive to the house is in a state of elegant neglect but still shows evidence of a former glory, and the slate bridge over Grisedale Beck is built in the traditional walling style with a picturesquely uneven castellation made from vertical slates of different lengths. The clear, bubbling stream has its origins high up in Grisedale Tarn and runs by a dense growth of conifers, rhododendrons and birches. At each corner of the bridge is a bell-shaped stone mounted on a pillar which gives a dignity to the approach to the house, now owned by the YMCA and used as an outdoor activity centre for young people.

From 1824 the Hall was owned by William Marshall, the eldest son of John Marshall from nearby Hallsteads and Member of Parliament for successively Petersfield, Beverley, Carlisle and East Cumberland; his father and brother were also MPs. It was in the Marshalls' period at the Hall that the Wordsworths came to know the building well, William staying there on at least one occasion and visiting the Hall on a number of others. Both Patterdale Hall and Hallsteads made a convenient break for him on his journeys to and from Lowther Castle.

The church we now see was built after Wordsworth's death, replacing an older Tudor chapel. Inside are two framed paintings of the church the Wordsworths knew.

It was on the way to Patterdale that Dorothy made a fascinating observation about a particular kind of rainy mist. Here she is on her pony, with William on foot: 'As we went along the mist gathered upon the valleys, and it even rained all the way to the head of Patterdale; but there was never a drop upon my habit larger than the smallest pearls upon a lady's ring.' Had they existed in her day, she might have resorted to a metaphor involving aerosol sprays, though her own image is decidedly more graphic.

Two miles further along the road from Glenridding, just beyond the road junction to Dockray, is a spot no one should miss if they are anxious to tread in the steps of Wordsworth. From the car-park on the left, cross the road and climb over a stile and onto a path which goes down to the lakeshore. This, as the National Trust sign announces, is Gowbarrow, the scene which inspired the 'daffodil poem'.

It comes as a surprise to many people to learn that Wordsworth was not in fact wandering alone on the shores of Ullswater but was accompanied by his sister Dorothy when he saw the famous daffodils. It comes as an even greater surprise for many to learn also that he did not, as he usually did, compose this verse extempore 'on location'. He wrote it some two years after seeing the daffodils at Gowbarrow on Thursday 15 April 1802, and he clearly drew heavily on Dorothy's own description of those hosts of golden daffodils, a description which *was* written immediately on the spot and which, quite apart from any association with her brother's more famous poem, deserves to be included in any anthology of fine prose:

> . . . when we were in the woods byond Gowbarrow Park we saw a few daffodils close to the water side. We fancied that the lake had floated the seeds ashore and that the little colony had so sprung up. But as we went along there were more and yet more and at last under the boughs of the trees, we saw that there was a long belt of them along the shore, about the breadth of a country turnpike road. I never saw daffodils so beautiful. They grew among the mossy stones about and about them, some rested their heads upon these stones as on a pillow for weariness and the rest tossed and reeled and danced and seemed as if they verily laughed with the wind that blew upon them over the lake, they looked so gay ever glancing ever changing. . . .

Two of the most effective lines in the poem were also contributed by William's wife, Mary:

> They flash upon that inward eye
> Which is the bliss of solitude. . . .

Today one would be fortunate indeed to see 'hosts' of daffodils, but with luck and careful timing, it is possible at least to see a respectable number, and at any time of the year there are splendid views across the lake. But in the spring there are joys in the area which, unrecorded in Wordsworth's much-memorized verse, did not escape his sister's keen eye for detail: the hawthorns 'black and green', the primroses, the wood sorrel, the scentless violets and '. . . that starry yellow flower which Mrs C. calls pile wort', presumably the lesser celandine, a small flower related to the common buttercup and which was the subject of some of Wordsworth's most inspired verse, as well as some of his most mediocre. The poem beginning 'There is a Flower, the lesser Celandine . . .' was written in the same year that he composed 'I wandered lonely as a cloud' and shows his 'nature poetry' at its best: not simply descriptive pretty verse but elevated to a higher plane of thought and feeling as the celandine becomes a symbol for man as he grows older and begins to experience the vicissitudes and disappointments of life:

> To be a Prodigal's Favourite – then, worse truth,
> A miser's Pensioner – behold our lot!
> O Man, that from thy fair and shining youth
> Age might but take the things Youth needed not!

Another much-loved poem belonging to this area was written in 1836, when Wordsworth was in his sixty-sixth year. This is his 'Airey Force Valley', approached from the car-park on the opposite side of the road from the lake. At any time of the year this valley is worth exploring, but after a few days of rain the waterfalls are always impressive. A stiff walk from the car-park along a well-defined route brings us to the falls themselves. A fine vantage-point is the bridge across Aira Beck, from which to imbibe the atmosphere created by the poem, which is concerned as much with what can be heard as what can be seen. A sense of timelessness pervades the whole scene, and the

> . . . brook itself,
> Old as the hills that feed it from afar,
> Doth rather deepen than disturb the calm . . .

until a tiny breeze, 'Escaped from boisterous winds that rage without', touches an ash and:

> . . . makes
> A soft eye-music of slow waving boughs,
> Powerful almost as vocal harmony
> To stay the wanderer's steps and soothe his thoughts.

This is also the setting for 'The Somnambulist', a strongly rhymed ballad-type poem with all the ingredients associated with Victorian melodramas. There is the beautiful maiden, hopeful suitors, a devoted knight, an heroic rescue and a tearful death.

Nearby is Lyulph's Tower (not open to the public), occasionally mentioned in letters, poems and journals. It

is large enough to be seen clearly from the far side of
Ullswater. This Gothic tower was built by the Duke of
Norfolk in 1780 as a hunting box. Wordsworth records
an occasion when he was passing this way *en route* for
Lowther Castle when Lady Lonsdale stopped her carriage and took him on board. Hitch-hiking, it seems, is
not entirely a twentieth-century activity.

In a famous passage in 'The Prelude' the boy William
steals a boat and takes it out into the lake for a moonlight
row. Literary detectives have for generations amused
themselves by trying to identify the precise location described in the verse, even in their frustration refusing to
accept his own assertion that it was 'by the shores of
Patterdale' and suggesting that Esthwaitewater was
really the lake concerned. The description, however,
could indeed be Ullswater, and Stybarrow Crag in many
respects fits the bill. In any event it is a fine description:

>   . . . lustily
> I dipp'd my oars into the silent Lake,
> And as I rose upon the stroke, my Boat
> Went heaving through the water, like a Swan;
> When from behind that craggy steep, till then
> The bound of the horizon, a huge Cliff
> As if with voluntary power instinct,
> Uprear'd its head. I struck, and struck again,
> And, growing still in stature, the huge cliff
> Rose up between me and the stars, and still,
> With measur'd motion, like a living thing,
> Strode after me. . . .

Barely three miles further along the lakeside road, in
the direction of Pooley Bridge, is Skelly Nab, on which are
two houses known intimately by the Wordsworths –
Hallsteads and Old Church. Hallsteads is now one of the
two Lakeland bases for the Outward Bound School, which
arranges adventure courses for young people. Although
the house and estate are private, it is possible to view the
grounds with written permission. The house was built in
1815 and was the home of the Wordsworths' lifelong

friends the Marshalls, whom they frequently visited and often stayed with. John Marshall and his son James accompanied Wordsworth on his Irish tour in 1826, and the table at Rydal Mount was often graced by fine vegetables from the kitchen garden of the estate. At least one Christmas turkey came from the Marshalls, and there are also references in Dorothy's letters to Hallsteads' fine apples and 'Long black skinned kidney potatoes . . . the best potatoes in the world'.

The Marshalls also had a home in Leeds, and one winter Dorothy tried to tempt them to spend some of their time at Ullswater with the prospect of 'a Christmas fire at Hallsteads with a view from the window of Helvellyn'. From the bay window on the first floor was the view which had so impressed her. Catstycam and Helvellyn summit were capped with cloud, but still alluring enough, one would have thought, to tempt anyone away from Leeds, and across the lake a fine panorama which included Hallin Fell and Place Fell.

Next door to Hallsteads is Old Church, now a country house hotel but also owned in Wordsworth's time by the Marshalls and inhabited by the Marshall sisters as a kind of 'family annexe'. Dorothy would often on her visits spend time with the sisters, who were probably responsible for the famed vegetables.

The house was built in 1754 and takes its name from the ancient church which occupied this lakeside site from the twelfth century. In 1558 the records tell of a new church being consecrated, and this was replaced eventually by the church under nearby Priest's Crag. According to Clark's *Survey of the Lakes*, the gigantic yew tree marks the spot where the church once stood. Wordsworth, that great planter of yews, must have often admired this particular specimen, as well as the smaller ones growing close by. The old photographs in the hotel's collection depict these distinctive trees.

The rooms of the hotel are furnished in the style of a private country residence; the neat and tidy lawn goes right down to the shore, and there are well-cared-for displays of heathers and rockery plants, as well as the ubiquitous rhododendrons and bedding schemes. This peaceful scene recalls Dorothy's poem, written in her later life but looking back to the days when she and Jane Marshall (née Pollard) shared their dreams of

> A cottage in a verdant dell
> A pure unsullied household well,
> A garden stored with fruit and flowers
> And sunny seats and shady bowers
> A file of hives for humming bees
> Under a row of stately trees . . .
> Such was the scene I fondly framed
> When life was new and hope untamed. . . .

Before the Marshalls built Hallsteads, they lived at Watermillock, and it was there that Dorothy was staying in December 1812 when her little nephew Thomas died of measles and inflammation of the lungs, just six months after his sister Catherine had died. Although Dorothy had spent a happy fortnight at Watermillock, she later acknowledged that the death of Thomas prevented her ever looking back on that period without sadness.

From Old Church the main road goes past Leeming House (another exceptionally fine country house hotel built in 1847 and set in some of the most impressive gardens to be found anywhere in the Lake District) to the hamlet of Watermillock. Turning left here, away from the lake shore, a country lane goes over Pencilmill Beck and climbs up to Watermillock Church, built in the shadow of Priest's Crag. The present church of All Saints was consecrated in 1884 and is on the site of a church dating as far back as 1558. The churchyard has many interesting stones, including a table tomb containing the remains of members of the Marshall family, among the Wordsworths' longest and closest friends. Jane Marshall was Dorothy's childhood friend, and Dorothy's first known letters are exchanges with her.

The setting of the church in such a quiet position and so close to the intriguingly named Priest's Crag is very picturesque, and it is worth visiting for that alone. There are, however, other items of interest, apart from the Marshall–Pollard connections. An unusual sundial is mounted on a red sandstone plinth, which is clearly much older than the brass dial. The carvings in the stone have been badly eroded, and it is therefore not possible to discern their significance.

Much clearer is an engraved stone which reminds us that the Wordsworths and their contemporaries were fortunate indeed if they received satisfactory medical treatment. Children and adults alike were often subjected to quite barbarous 'cures': there are many references in their letters to the particularly obnoxious 'blistering' method of curing illnesses. Consequently it is pleasing to find in this remote churchyard evidence of at least one successful medical practitioner who must have brought relief to many in the area: the stone records that John William Benjamin Taylor 'was an eminent and successful bone setter equalled by few, and not perhaps surpassed by any in his time, having exemplified in his practice the art of replacing broken and dislocated bones in every part of the human body'. Such people were genuinely revered in their time for curing illnesses and complaints which to-day, with access to marvellous antibiotics, we think of as hardly more than minor inconveniences. The eye complaint that so often made Wordsworth wretched in his later years was cured by the application of a 'blue stone', actually of copper sulphate. He wrote from nearby Hall-steads in 1826 to thank the acquaintance who had introduced this cure to him, describing how the '. . . stone was applied by Mrs W to my eyes, five or six times; it distressed them not a little for a time; but they have not been any thing like so well for many years as since.' Perhaps in some distant churchyard there is a tombstone recording the esteem in which the unknown apothecary was held who first thought of the copper sulphate treatment and brought relief to many sufferers.

Park House near Dalemain on the road from Pooley Bridge to Stainton was taken by Mary Wordsworth's brother Tom Hutchinson from 1804 to 1808. Tom's sisters, Sara and Joanna, kept house for him. During this time all the Wordsworths were frequent guests at the house.

Although there is no public road by the farm itself, two parallel paths go in front of and behind the house and make a fine circular walk in an area where most tourists confine their attentions to Ullswater. The lower path begins at Dalemain and continues from the road and around the back of this gracious mansion. Once beyond the Dalemain buildings, the track levels out and follows the 500-foot contour. Immediately on the left a track leads off the right of way at right angles and climbs the hillside to a farm: this is Park House, which comes into better view further along the route, clearly profiled against the sky on an exposed slope some six hundred feet above sea-level. A single avenue of trees, planted in a dead straight line, defines the track to the right, and below, to the left, is the Dacre Beck. No longer can the building be aptly described as a 'white house on a hill', but one can still appreciate why the Hutchinsons had such a hard time of it trying to farm these exposed and sloping fields. The route makes an exhilarating and bracing walk, but few would like to spend a full winter up here. Soon the way turns from the valley side and climbs towards and past Dacre Castle, which at first sight from the approach looks every inch the kind of cut-out model of a fort a child might make. This impressive fortification dates from the early fourteenth century and can be visited by written appointment. The track comes out onto the road at Dacre village, and a further lane to the right leads to Dacre Church, which is rich in history.

When Dorothy arrived here in May 1804, she met Mary's brother and sister, Tom and Sara Hutchinson, just as they were coming out of the church. On this fine day of early summer they must have rejoiced with Dorothy at the fields which 'looked delightfully green and the place altogether exceedingly pleasant'. Surely they must have also observed the curious and engaging figures of the four carved stone bears, set at the four corners of the church-yard. Mystery still surrounds these figures, but a most convincing theory has been put forward that the story unfolds in an anti-clockwise direction, beginning with the sleeping bear in the north-west corner. This figure is particularly badly worn, but on the next stone it is obvious that another animal, possibly a cat or lynx, has jumped on the bear's back. Next the bear seems to be trying to shake off the cat, and finally the unfortunate cat seems to have been eaten by the bear, whose smug, self-satisfied and well-fed appearance is now unmistakable – once the idea has been suggested. Strange that Dorothy, with her keen eye for such details, does not comment on these Dacre bears, but perhaps she was more preoccupied with helping the Hutchinsons to settle in their new home.

Although much involved with fitting up beds and curtains, she still had time to take some 'delightful walks', and on one occasion got very wet crossing Dacre Beck due to its 'miserable stepping-stones'. In her fortnight's stay she came to like the area very much indeed, but she continued to regret that Park House had been built so high on the hill, a fact still surprising today, since Lakeland builders normally show great skill in choosing the correct aspect for sun and shelter.

A path goes in front of the churchyard wall on the opposite side of the field from Dacre Castle, but running parallel with the earlier path for a short while. When Dorothy came this way, she must surely have noticed the cress growing in the running water of the tiny stream. The church is seen to advantage on the left, whilst the castle commands our attention on the right. It was one of a series of fortified pele towers erected during the Border raids between Scotland and England. The impressive walls are sixty-six feet high, and the battlements have been remarkably well preserved. It is again inhabited and has enjoyed a long history. Dorothy's description of the area in 1802 remains accurate today: 'The trees are left scattered about as if intended to be like a park, and these are very interesting, standing as they do upon the sides of the steep hills that slope down to the Bed of the River, a little stony-bedded stream that spreads out to a considerable breadth at the village of Dacre.'

Ascending the gently sloping field back towards Park

House, it is worth casting a backward glance to enjoy the unusual views of Dunmallet (Dunmallard on OS maps) and Blencathra. A ladder stile gives access to a field which may contain some friendly fell ponies, and crossing this pasture, a most unusual four-storey bank barn can be seen high on the right. Although the footpath leads behind Park House, it is still possible to gain some idea of the aspect the farm enjoyed. But what an exposed position! Little wonder that on a January visit in 1805 Dorothy caught a cold and Mary suffered from toothache. However, Dorothy's constitution must have been strong, for two days after complaining of a cold so bad that she could barely open her eyes, she was happily walking with William to Hutton John.

The path now goes up a steep bank away from Park House towards the village of Stainton, where William's brother Richard (the London lawyer) invested in a field in 1805. (He already administered the family estate at the nearby hamlet of Sockbridge, on the other side of the River Eamont.) The path rejoins the road a short distance north of Dalemain, where this walk began. With luck the walker may have glimpsed the Dalemain deer, descendants of the very ones Dorothy admired.

Dalemain is frequently mentioned in letters and journals, but usually merely as the termination of a walk or as a landmark which one or other member of the family passed. Today it is regularly open to the public, one of the more recent of Lakeland's historic houses to welcome visitors. The Georgian front of the house conceals an even more fascinating building, going back some eight centuries to its origins as a pele tower – part of the line of Border defences which included Dacre Castle, a fact which makes it particularly appropriate as the home of the Westmorland and Cumberland Yeomanry Museum.

Inside the house the elegant drawing-rooms and fine dining-room are redolent of the more gracious life of the eighteenth century, whilst the family portraits of the Hassels speak eloquently of their three-hundred-year association with the house.

The garden would certainly have greatly interested the

Wordsworths had they been allowed access to it. There are rare trees and unusual old-fashioned trees and shrubs which produce strong fragrances. The knot garden with its low, clipped, boxwood hedges was planted in Elizabethan times, and in the great sixteenth-century barn is a museum devoted to the fell pony, Lakeland's own native breed. The home-made teas are served not, as is often the case, in austere stable blocks but in a medieval hall, which often boasts a large log fire. Under these circumstances, it is easy to recreate a picture of life at the neighbouring Park House in the New Year of 1805, when Dorothy wrote '. . . we have just put our two children to bed and William, Mary, Sara, Joanna, Tom, and George Hutchinson with Hartley Coleridge are making a Christmas Party round the fire. . . .'

Let us leave them there by the warmth of their Park House fire, to enjoy a richly deserved festival, sheltered from the wintry winds without, fortified by the knowledge that, although many sad events lie ahead of them, there will also be many uplifting moments among these hills and dales:

> The innocent brightness of a new-born Day
> > Is lovely yet;
> The clouds that gather round the setting sun
> Do take a sober colouring from an eye
> That hath kept watch o'er man's mortality;
> Another race hath been, and other palms are won.
> Thanks to the human heart by which we live,
> Thanks to its tenderness, its joys, and fears,
> To me the meanest flower that blows can give
> Thoughts that do often lie too deep for tears.

Epilogue

The idea for this book first came to me in an idle and almost hypnotic moment in the drawing-room – library at Rydal Mount. It was a wild autumn evening outside and the blazing log fire was a cheerful prospect after the bleak journey to the Mount at the invitation of the Custodians, Christine and Don Brookes. They had lit the room with candles and withdrawn to prepare for their expected guests. I was alone by the very fireside which members of the Wordsworth family had enjoyed for half a century. As I glanced around at the portraits hanging on the walls in the flickering candlelight, I realized that among the enormous volume of writings about the Wordsworths there was still a story to be told: the story of their work and lives among one of the most beautiful landscapes in the world. I thus began this *Portrait of the Wordsworth Country* surrounded by the portraits of the people who were to occupy many of my sleeping as well as waking moments for the next twenty-two months. The final pages were composed in very different circumstances; they were completed on the island in the middle of Grasmere during one of the finest English summers in living memory. The contrasting surroundings in which this book was started and finished sum up for me the greatest quality of the 'Wordsworth Country' – its almost unbelievable variety and richness. It has been a privilege to glimpse some of

194

that richness and variety and now to lay down my pen to
experience with Wordsworth:

> The silence that is in the starry sky
> The sleep that is among the lonely hills.

Bibliography

I have found the following books invaluable in preparing this work for publication:

Wordsworth: Poetical Works, edited by Thomas Hutchinson, revised by Ernest de Selincourt, Oxford University Press, first published 1904, new edition 1936

Wordsworth's Guide to the Lakes (1835), edited and introduced by Ernest de Selincourt, Oxford University Press, first published 1906

Wordsworth: The Prelude, text of 1805 edited with introduction and notes by Ernest de Selincourt, Oxford University Press, first published 1933, revised by Helen Darbishire in 1960

The Letters of William and Dorothy Wordsworth, first edited by Ernest de Selincourt and published by Oxford University Press in six volumes 1935–1939; extensively revised and rearranged in seven volumes as follows:

   I *The Early Years 1797–1805*, edited by Chester L. Shaver (1967)

  II *The Middle Years, Part 1, 1806–1811*, edited by Mary Moorman (1969)

 III *The Middle Years, Part 2, 1812–1820*, edited by Mary Moorman & Alan G. Hill (1970)

 IV *The Later Years, Part 1, 1821–1828*, edited by Alan G. Hill (1978)

  V *The Later Years, Part 2, 1829–1834*, edited by Alan G. Hill (1979)

VI *The Later Years, Part 3, 1835–1839*, edited by Alan G. Hill (1982)

VII *The Later Years, Part 4, 1840–1850*, edited by Alan G. Hill (forthcoming)

Journals of Dorothy Wordsworth, edited by Mary Moorman, Oxford University Press (1973)

William Wordsworth: A Biography, by Mary Moorman: I *The Early Years*, Oxford University Press (1967) II *The Later Years*, Oxford University Press (1965)

William Wordsworth, by Hunter Davies, Weidenfeld & Nicolson (1980)

The King's England – Lake Counties, by Arthur Mee, Hodder & Stoughton (1969)

The Buildings of England, by Nikolaus Pevsner, Penguin Books, *Cumberland and Westmorland* (1967) *North Lancashire* (1969)

Life and Tradition in the Lake District, by William Rollinson, Dalesman Books (1981)

Grasmere and the Wordsworths, by W. R. Mitchell, Dalesman Books (1973)

Cumbria, by John Parker, Bartholomew (1977)

Transactions of the Cumberland & Westmorland Antiquarian & Archaeological Society, published annually, Titus Wilson, Kendal (1962, 1964, 1971, 1975, 1976)

Cockermouth, by J. Bernard Bradbury, Phillimore (1981)

Wordsworth at Colthouse, by Eileen Jay, Titus Wilson, Kendal (1970)

Greta Hall, by H. W. Howe with revisions by Robert Woof, Daedalus Press, Norfolk (1977)

The Discovery of the Lake District 1750–1810, by Peter Bicknell and Robert Woof, Trustees of Dove Cottage, Grasmere (1982)

The Lake District Discovered 1810–1850, by Peter Bicknell and Robert Woof, Trustees of Dove Cottage, Grasmere (1983)

The Wordsworth Circle, by Robert Woof, Trustees of Dove Cottage, Grasmere (1979)

William Wordsworth, by Ronald Sands, Pitkin Pictorials (1981)

Wordsworthshire, by Eric Robertson, Chatto & Windus (1911)

The Lake District: An Anthology, by Norman Nicholson, Robert Hale (1977), Penguin Books (1978)

Index